CREATIVE
CLOTH
DOLL
COUTURE

QUARRY

To my two fashion consultants, Janet Beth Cruz and Heidi Culea— two of the best daughters anyone could have.

First published in the United States of America by

Quarry Books, a member of
Quayside Publishing Group
33 Commercial Street
Gloucester, Massachusetts 01930-5089
Telephone: (978) 282-9590
Fax: (978) 283-2742
www.rockpub.com

Library of Congress Cataloging-in-Publication Data
Medaris Culea, Patti.
    Creative cloth doll couture : new approaches to making
    beautiful clothing and accessories / Patti Medaris Culea.
        p.   cm.
    ISBN 1-59253-217-9 (pbk.)
    1. Doll clothes—Patterns. 2. Dress accessories. I. Title.
    TT175.7.M43 2006
    745.592'21—dc22   2005030580

ISBN 1-59253-217-9

10 9 8 7 6 5 4 3 2 1

Design: Dutton & Sherman Design
Cover Image and Photography: Bob Hirsch
Gallery Photography: Allan Penn Photography
Technical Editor: Susan Huxley
Copy Editor: Katherine O. Riess
Illustrations: Judy Love
Patterns: Roberta Frauwirth

Printed in Singapore

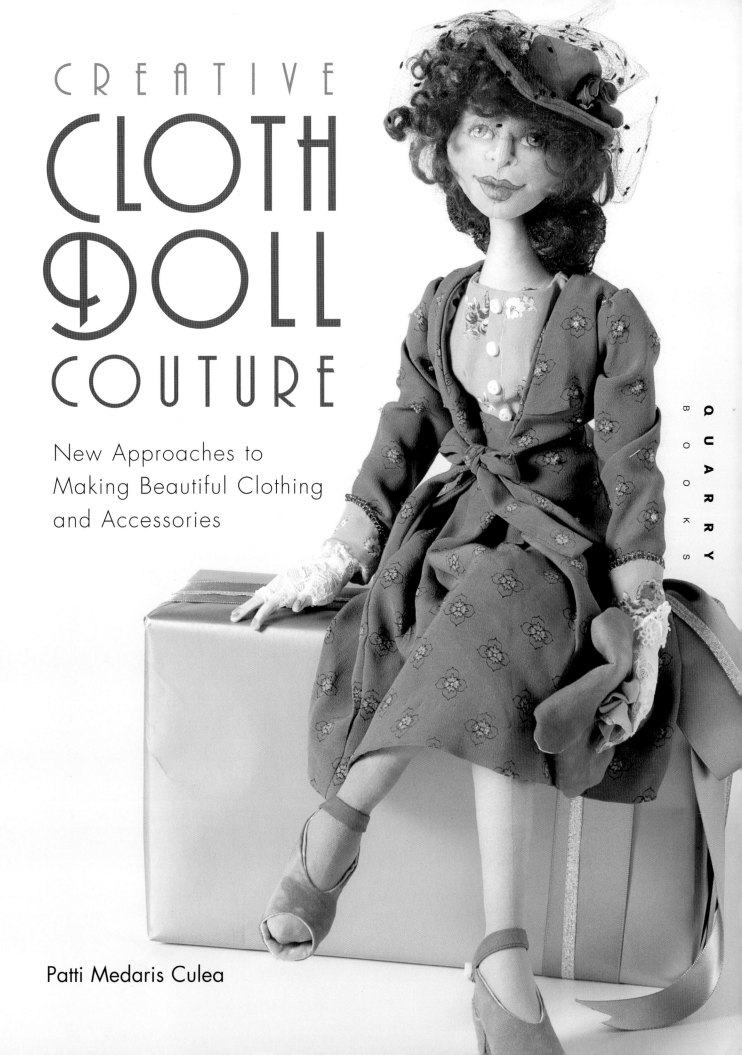

CREATIVE
CLOTH
DOLL
COUTURE

New Approaches to
Making Beautiful Clothing
and Accessories

GLOUCESTER MASSACHUSETTS

QUARRY BOOKS

Patti Medaris Culea

CONTENTS

ꟾNTRODUCTION

Before we go too far, first things first. Couture (pronounced ku-tur) is a dusty word, early twentieth century to be exact, that I hope will become like an old friend. The word means to design, make, or sell fashionable women's clothing. In this book, we will apply new creative techniques to create wonderful clothing for our cloth dolls.

When you first encounter someone, your gaze typically moves from the face to the hair, and then to the clothing and accessories. With dolls, it is no different. Doll fashion is just as important as human fashion. After we breathe, eat, and dream about our doll's body and face, making the clothes and accessories is the frosting on our artwork.

Human couture tends to stay with the basics. Doll couture has no limits. It can be whimsical and unbelievably out of proportion—anything we want. Our dolls can be clothed in fibers you would never see on a human, and they never worry about being seen in the same outfit twice. There are no restrictions when you make your way along the doll couture imagination superhighway.

It is my hope that this book will spark imagination, creativity, and enjoyment when you are designing your doll's wardrobe. Beyond that, I am certain you will find out how easy it is to change the patterns to suit your wildest ideas, and give you the confidence to do so.

Bon couture!

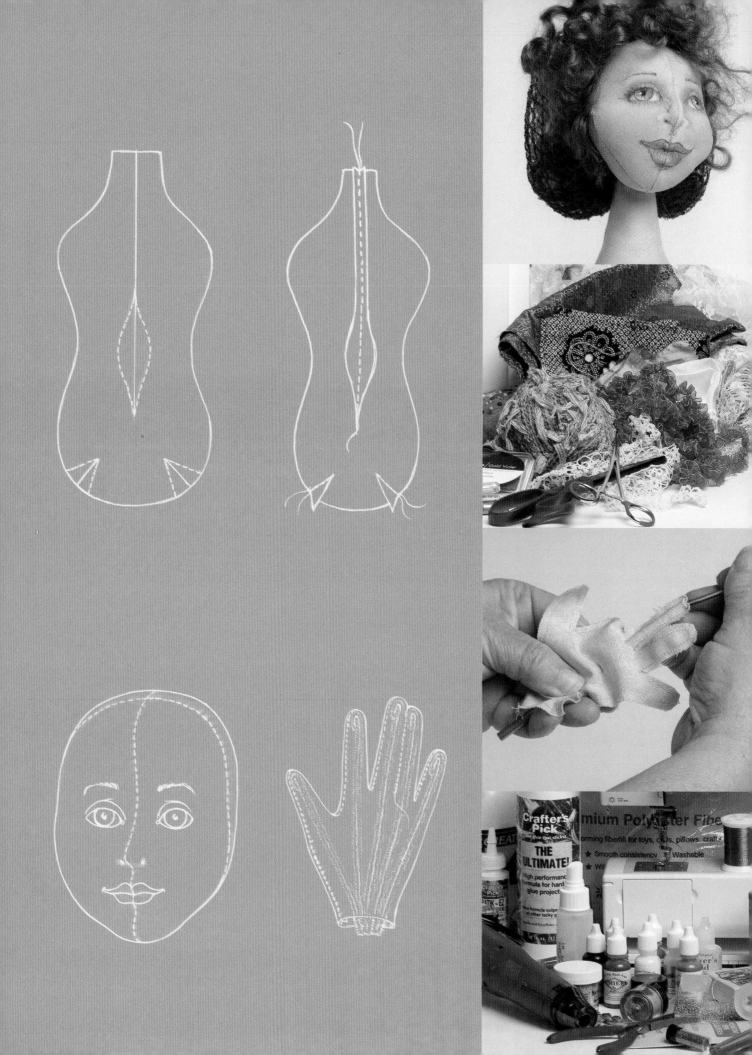

CHAPTER 1

THE BASIC BODY: CONSTRUCTING THE MODEL DOLL

The goal of this book is to show how to create funky, glamorous, realistic, and whimsical clothing and accessories, but first, we need a body to work on. In this chapter, you will learn how to sew together a basic cloth body, sculpt and draw a face, and along the way, become familiar with some basic supplies and sewing techniques.

The Basic Body pattern in this book makes an 18" (45.7 cm) -tall cloth doll. This is the perfect size for a fashion doll. By working your way through the projects in this book, you will have options for making a wardrobe that is removable or permanently secured to her body.

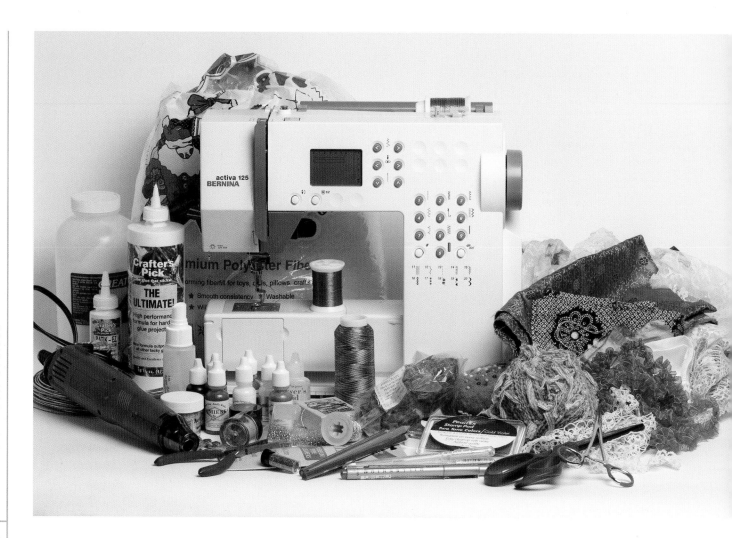

THE BASIC BODY KIT

⅓ yard (30.5 cm) of white or light-colored 100% cotton fabric

colored pencils: light or sienna brown for shading; lighter tan, beige, or flesh for highlights; white for pronounced highlights; carmine red for cheeks; light, medium, and dark colors for eyes; two shades of pink, red, or rose for lips

fabric pens: black, brown, contrasting color for the eyes, red white gel pen

6 pipe cleaners for wiring fingers

stuffing such as Fairfield Poly-fil strong thread for sculpting and attaching arms and legs, color-matched to fabric

textile medium such as Createx Textile Medium or JoSanja Textile Medium

thread to match fabric

soft fabric eraser such as Magic Rub

mechanical pencil

clear plastic quilter's gridded ruler

template plastic (optional)

stuffing tools

sewing machine

turning tools such as the Itsy Bitsy Finger Turning kit or small brass tubes (see Resources, page 120)

needle-nose pliers

wire cutters

THE BASIC SEWING KIT

sewing machine

sewing machine needles: universal points in size 10 and 12; embroidery, metallic, and top stitch in size 12

hand-sewing needles (sharps, milliners, quilter's basting needles, darners, embroidery, chenille)

3" (7.6 cm) -long doll-sculpting needle

size 11/12 beading needle

variety of sewing machine presser feet, such as darning, open-toed, and zigzag

sewing machine tools (for changing needles, oiling, and cleaning)

seam ripper

iron

press cloth

small bottle of Sewer's Aid

extra bobbins

beading threads

straight pins

safety pins

pincushion

thimble

cutting rulers

measuring tape

template plastic (optional)

rotary cutter and self-healing cutting board (optional)

straight-edge fabric scissors

embroidery scissors

paper scissors

pinking shears

hemostats (hand-held surgical clamps) or forceps

large and small tools for turning fingers

stuffing fork

seed beads in various sizes and colors

crystals

accent and drop beads

pencil

small scratch pad

journal

THE BASIC FABRIC-DYEING KIT

Jacquard Dye-Na-Flow paints

Jacquard Pearl-EX pigments

Jacquard Textile Paints

Jacquard Lumiere Paints

Jacquard Silk Dyes

Jacquard Procion MX powder dyes

noniodized salt

Tsukineko Fantastix

Tsukineko Brilliance stamp pads

Tsukineko all-purpose inks

several sizes of soft, flat, and round paint brushes for applying dyes and paints

containers for mixing dyes, such as a plastic ice cube tray

container for water

painter's masks for working with powdered dyes

paper toweling

plastic to cover work surface

TIP

There are many types and brands of colored pencils. They all work fine on cloth, but the best are oil based. These include Sanford Prismacolor (Karisma internationally), Walnut Hollow Oil Pencils, and Van Gogh Colored Pencils.

THE BASIC CLOTHING KIT

cotton batik fabrics

synthetic fabrics such as polyester organza, polyester silkies

silk fabrics such as chiffon, crepe de Chine, dupioni, sand-washed charmeuse

other fabrics such as bridals, brocades, fancies, rayons, tulle or fine netting

paper towels or pattern drafting paper

variegated and metallic sewing machine threads

lace

trims

silk ribbons

wire-edged ribbon

BASIC SEWING TIPS

- No matter when you last used your sewing machine, it is best to clean and oil it before you start a new project. If you do this often, your sewing machine, no matter how new or old it is, will serve you for years and years.

- Machine needles are another important piece of equipment. Always insert a new needle into the machine for each project. Make sure you have the proper size and type of needle for the fabric and thread. The suitable needle type is listed in each chapter under Materials.

- You may want to dye the fabric for the body. If so, white or light-colored cotton is the best fabric for your doll.

- Make templates of the pattern pieces you will be working with. Transfer all of the markings onto the templates. Place the templates in a zippered plastic bag.

- Some pattern pieces, such as the hands and face, are best traced directly from the patterns, rather than using templates. Use a light table or window to trace these pieces accurately. Other pattern pieces are sewn together before the shapes are cut from the seamed fabric layers. For this process, it is best to first use straight-edge fabric scissors to cut out the general shape from the fabric pieces. Then, after the pieces are sewn, use pinking shears to cut out the detailed shape. By using the pinking shears, you will not need to clip curves. Do not use pinking shears to cut out the face and hands, however. These pieces are too small and need a more accurate cutting technique.

- Seam allowances can be finger pressed open or ironed. This is strictly up to each individual. Some of the seams do not have to be pressed open. Doll makers are not as precise as seamstresses or quilters. We tend to go with the flow.

THE BODY CONSTRUCTION

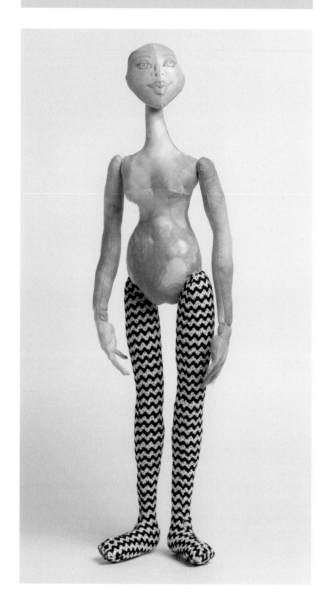

In this book, there is one body pattern and two variations for the legs. On pages 108–109, you will find three leg patterns. Two pattern pieces are the upper and lower legs for a sitting figure and another pattern piece is for a standing figure. The pattern pieces give you options for the pose you want for the various outfits. Because the focus of this book is on clothing and accessories, the body has a model-type shape. The wardrobe you create will look beautiful on her long, curvy figure. In a sense, you are making your own high-fashion doll with an exciting, fun, and varied wardrobe. Your doll will have something to wear for every occasion.

1. Before starting your doll, note the pattern pieces that need to be traced onto fabric, cut to the rough shape, and then sewn before cutting them out precisely: the Face, Head Back, Ear (Fairy only, see Golendrial, page 86), Arm, Hand, and leg pieces (Upper Leg and Lower Leg for the sitting doll, or Straight Leg for the standing doll). The main body pieces are cut out in detail, and then sewn together. See the Face, Head Back, and optional Ear pattern pieces (page 107).

2. All pattern pieces are templates, meaning you trace them on the wrong side of the fabric with the mechanical pencil. You can use a light table to trace directly from the pattern pieces to the fabric. Or, you can trace the pieces onto template plastic, place the template plastic shapes on the wrong side of the fabric, and trace around them. Trace darts and openings, too. Trace the head pieces onto the wrong side of one half of the fabric, making sure you match the on-grain arrows to the lengthwise grain of the fabric. The grainline is only important for the head.

3. Double the fabric by folding it in half, right sides together. Pin the layers together in several places. Sew seam #1 on the Face. Sew seam #2 on the Head Back, leaving open for turning where marked. With the straight-edge fabric scissors, cut out the two pieces, using full 1/8" (3 mm) seam allowances. Open them up.

> **TIP**
>
> *On my Bernina sewing machine, a normal stitch length is 2.0. I lower the setting for a shorter stitch length of 1.8 or 1.5 when sewing the face and fingers so that I have clean, strong seams.*

4. With right sides together, pin the Head Back to the Face at the top and the chin.

5. Sew all the way around the pieces to complete seam #3 (figure a). Turn the joined pieces through the opening on the Head Back, and fill the shape with enough stuffing to make the head firm. Set the head aside.

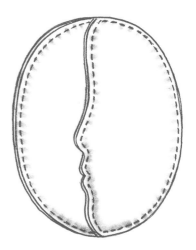

(figure a)
Sew the face to the back of the head.

6. With the fabric doubled, trace and then cut out all of the pattern pieces for the body (page 107), using straight-edge fabric scissors. Mark the darts (figure b).

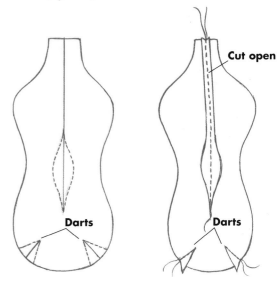

(figure b)
Make darts in Body Back and Lower Body Front.

7. On the Body Back, cut down the center of the back where marked, from the neck down to the hip. Sew in the darts on the Body Back and Lower Body Front.

8. Fold the Body Back in half, right sides together. Starting at the neck on the Body Back, sew down to the opening then continue sewing from the lower part of the opening, curving where marked. This creates a nice curve to the doll's spine. Double stitch the beginning of the neck.

9. Pin the Upper Body Front to the Lower Body Front, starting at the center of the bust and working out to each side. Sew from the center of the bust out to one side (figure c). Repeat on the opposite side of the bust.

(figure c)
Join Body Front pieces at bustline.

10. With right sides together and using a full ¹/₈" (3 mm) seam allowance, pin the body front to the Body Back, and sew around the sides, from the neck opening down the body and around up to the other side of the neck. Trim the seam allowances with pinking shears. Turn the body right side out by inserting the hemostats into the body, grabbing the end of a body part, and then pulling it through the center back opening. Smooth out the curves with the closed end of the hemostats. Fill the body with stuffing. Plump up the breasts with the stuffing. Set the body aside.

TIP

It is easier to fill up the body until the stuffing starts to pop out of the opening in the back and then close the opening with a ladder stitch (page 119). It helps to insert a pipe cleaner into the neck before filling the neck with stuffing. This keeps the head from getting wobbly.

11. Trace two arms onto the wrong side of the fabric. Fold the fabric in half, right sides together. Back stitching at the beginning and end of the seam, sew from the opening at the wrist all the way around. Leave an opening at the wrist. Cut out the arms with pinking shears, leaving a full 1/8" (3 mm) seam allowance. Turn the arms right side out and fill them with stuffing to just below the elbow.

12. Trace two hands onto the wrong side of the fabric. Double the fabric, with right sides together. Carefully sew around the shape, leaving the wrist open (figure d). Be sure you make two stitches between each finger and two stitches across the tip of each finger. (Do not sew down the dashed lines for the attached fingers yet.)

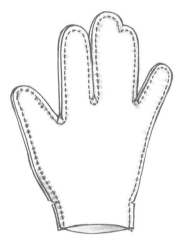

(figure d)
Using a short stitch, sew together the hand fabric layers before cutting out the shape.

13. Cut out the hands with a good pair of sharp scissors. Clip at each side between the fingers and right up to the stitches. This helps prevent wrinkling once the hands are turned. Turn the hands right side out, using brass tubes to help with the fingers (figure e).

(figure e)
Turn the fingers right side out using small and large brass tubes.

14. After the fingers are turned, topstitch down the center of the two fingers that are attached.

15. Using three pipe cleaners for each hand, wire the hands by folding each pipe cleaner in half and inserting one half up each finger. The straight pipe cleaner is inserted into the thumb. Wrap some of this pipe cleaner around the two used for the fingers to hold everything in place (figure f). Using a stuffing fork, fill just the palm side of each hand. Insert stuffing into the wrists, around the pipe cleaners.

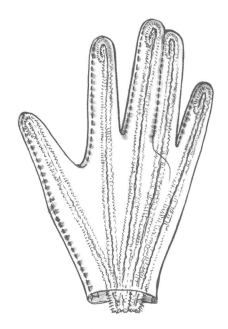

(figure f)
Sew between the joined fingers before inserting pipe cleaners and stuffing the hand.

16. Insert the top of a hand into the wrist of each arm. You will have a bit of the thumb pipe-cleaner sticking out of the wrist. Insert this bit of pipe-cleaner into the arm and finish filling up the arms around the wire. Use a ladder stitch (page 119) to sew the hands to the arms at the wrists. Set the arms aside.

17. Decide if your doll will have jointed or straight legs and follow the instructions below or on page 17.

OPTION 1: JOINTED LEGS

1. Trace two Upper Legs and two Lower Legs onto the wrong side of the fabric. Double the fabric, right sides together, and pin the layers together in several places. Sew all the way around both of the Upper Legs. Using full 1/8" (3 mm) seam allowances, cut out the shapes with pinking shears and cut a slit at the top, where marked. Turn the Upper Leg right side out through the slit and fill the shape with stuffing. Close up the slit by hand sewing using a needle and thread.

2. Sew the sides of the Lower Legs from the knee all the way down to the opening at the toes. Cut out the shapes, using full 1/8" (3 mm) seam allowances.

3. Fold a Lower Leg at the knees so that the front and back seams match. Sew across the top of the leg, through both fabric layers, stopping short of the matched seams so there is an opening at the center (figure g).

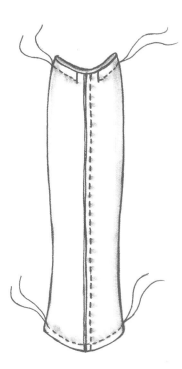

(figure g)
Refold the leg to seam the top and bottom edges.

4. For the feet, draw in a curved pencil line across the top area, as shown, and then sew the edges together following your drawn line (figure g).

5. Turn the Lower Leg right side out through the opening at the top, and fill the shape with stuffing. Close up the opening by hand sewing using a needle and thread.

6. Thread a 3" (7.6 cm) doll sculpting needle with 1/2 yard (46 cm) of strong thread and knot the end. Insert the needle through the top of a Lower Leg. Continue pulling the needle and thread through the Upper Leg at the dot. Go through the top of the remaining Lower Leg. Sew back and forth three times.

7. Continue assembling the doll following the steps for The Body Parts Assembly (page 18).

OPTION 2: STRAIGHT LEGS

1. Trace two legs onto the wrong side of one half of the fabric, and then double the fabric, right sides together. Sew from one side of the opening at the toes all the way around the foot and leg to the other side of the toe opening, using full 1/8" (3 mm) seam allowances. Cut out the shapes.

2. Fold the leg so that the front and back seams match and the toe area of the foot is flat and horizontal. For each foot, pin the toes together (figure h).

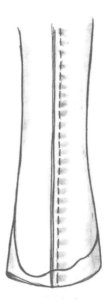

(figure h)
Join the straight leg pieces before seaming the toes.

3. Trace the foot template on page 109 onto the toe area. Sew along the traced lines. Trim the seam allowances with pinking shears. Finish the foot on the remaining leg in the same way.

4. Place the legs so that the feet face forward and cut a slit at the top of each leg on the sides that face each other. Turn through these openings and fill firmly with stuffing. Close up the slit by hand sewing.

The Body Parts Assembly

1. Attach a finished leg to each side of the body using 1 yard (91 cm) of strong thread and a long needle. Attach the thread at the hip, pull the needle and thread through the top of one leg from the inner side to the outer side, then turn the needle and insert it back through the same leg and through. Without breaking the thread, pull the needle and thread through the remaining leg to attach it in the same manner. Sew back and forth three times, and then anchor the thread at the hip, under a leg (figure i).

2. The arms are attached individually. Start by attaching the thread at the shoulder. Insert the needle and thread into—but not through—the arm. Push through just enough to catch some stuffing. Sew back into the shoulder. Go back and forth with the needle and thread three times. Anchor the thread off at the shoulder with a small stitch.

3. Hand sew the head to the neck using a needle and thread and a ladder stitch (page 119) (figure j).

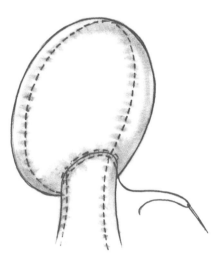

(figure j)
Hand sew the head to the neck.

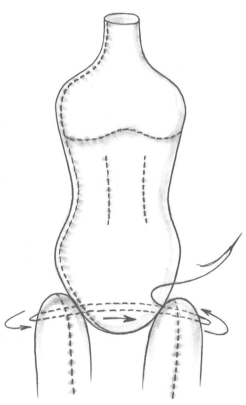

(figure i)
Join the upper legs to the body.

THE FACE GRID

1. Creating a grid will help you draw the face (figure k). The grid is simple to draw because you will use some reference points on the face to set it up. Follow the illustration as you draw the marks and lines with a mechanical pencil while going through the various steps.

The lengthwise seam on the face designates the center of the grid. To find the halfway point across the width, find the curve of the nose where it starts to shift out from the face, below the forehead. This is generally at the halfway point between the forehead and the chin. Place a pencil mark here, on either side of the center seam (#1).

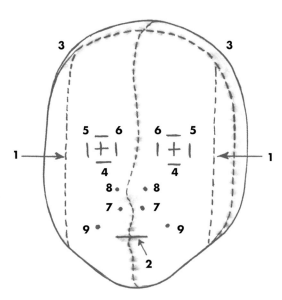

(figure k)
Grid for the face.

2. Below the bottom curve of the nose, find the halfway point between the nose and the chin. This is the center of the mouth. Place a mark here (#2).

3. To locate the center of the eyes, it is important to slice off a section of each side of the head. To find this, look at the head and find where the top of the head starts to curve outward. This is the temple area. Draw some dashed lines down each side of the head at these locations (#3).

4. Find the halfway point between one of these dashes and the center seam. Place a vertical pencil mark here (#4); it should fall on horizontal pencil mark #1. Make the same mark on the other side of the face.

5. For the width of each eye, you will half each of these halves. From the slice between #3 to #4, find the halfway point. Make a vertical pencil mark here (#5). Make the same mark on the other side of the face.

6. Halfway between #4 and the center seam of the face, make a pencil mark (#6). You now have one eye width between the marks for the inner corners of each eye. The distance between #5 and #6 is the width of an eye.

7. Measure the width of one eye. The height of an eye is the same as the width. Make a pencil mark above and below #1 for the eye height. Draw a square using the pencils marks as references. Imagine that you have drawn an eye socket for each side of the face. An eyeball will fit inside each square.

8. The nostrils are next. Find a slight inward curve on the face. On either side of the center seam and directly down from #6 (the inside corner of the eye), make a small dot with the pencil (#7). Do the same on the other side of the face.

9. The flare of the nose is straight up from the nostrils and halfway to the lower inside corner of the eye. Make a pencil mark on both sides of the center seam (#8).

10. The outside corners of the lips are in a direct line with #4. Make a small dot with the pencil (#9) on both sides of the face and in line with the center of the mouth (#2).

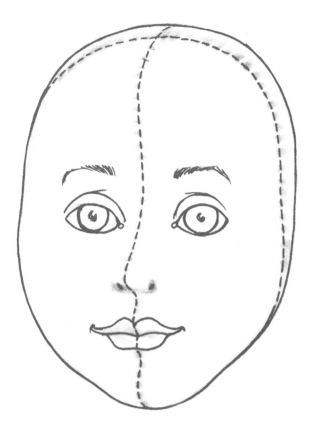

(figure l)
Features Illustration.

THE FEATURES

1. The features are very simple—mainly a series of circles. The eyes are three circles. Using a mechanical pencil, draw a large circle inside the square eye socket. Draw a medium-sized circle inside the first one, for the eyeball. Place a smaller circle in the center of the second one, for the iris. Note: The largest circle has been covered with the eyelids in the Features Illustration (figure l).

2. Draw the eyelids next. The upper eyelid starts just inside the largest circle (just outside the middle circle) and curves along the top, touching the middle circle (the iris). It stops on the outside of the eyeball, (the largest circle).

3. The lower eyelid connects to the inside edge of the upper eyelid, curves slightly down, and stops at the same place as the upper eyelid, on the outer edge of the eyeball (the largest circle).

4. The eyebrows are slightly above the square you drew earlier for the eye socket, above points #5 and #6 on the face grid (figure k). The inside of the eyebrow starts straight up from the inside of the eye, arches above the outer edge of the eyeball and ends just slightly out from the outer edge of the eyeball. Note: The nose will be sculpted so you need not worry about it for now.

5. The lips are a series of circles. Make a small one on the center seam for the turbuncle (or milkbud, the tiny circle in the center of the upper lip). On either side of this, draw larger circles, keeping them under the nose. Make the lower lip more of an oval shape.

6. Following the outer edges of the circles, outline the upper lip and lower lip and draw in the center of the lips.

7. With a brown fabric pen, outline the eyelids, iris, pupil, and lips. Erase all pencil marks except for the nostrils, flare, and eyebrows, which are drawn in steps 11 and 12 on page 23.

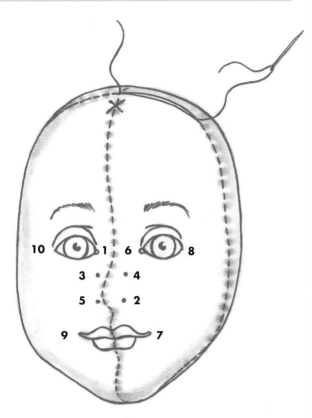

(figure m)
Sculpting Points Chart.

1. Thread the 3" (7.6 cm) long sculpting needle with 1 yard (91 cm) of strong thread. Knot one end of the thread. Anchor the thread by taking a stitch in the back of the head, behind the top seam. The knot will not show because the hair will cover it. Note: Without this small stitch, the knot might pop through the head and come out the front of the face. Refer to the Sculpting Points Chart above (figure m) as you work through the following steps.

2. Push the needle into the head and out at the inside corner of the eye (#1).

3. Go back into the head, but not too close to the place where you previously came out. This can be a vertical or horizontal stitch. Pull the needle and thread out at the opposite nostril (#2). From this point on, as you go in and out, start pulling on the thread to define the features. Keep the thread taut, but do not pull it too tightly, or you will create wrinkles. Look at the features as you sculpt, pulling tighter as needed. Shift the stuffing back into the nose while stitching. As you go in and out, dig down with your needle and catch quite a bit of stuffing between the needle and the surface of the head.

4. Insert the needle back into the head and pull it out the opposite side of the nose, at the flare (#3). Go back into the head and straight across to the other flare (#4).

5. Insert the needle into the head, down to the opposite nostril (#5), back into the head, and up to the opposite inside corner of the eye that was not stitched earlier (#6).

6. Working on the same side of the face throughout this step, insert the needle back into the head and down to the outside corner of the mouth (#7). Go back into the head and up to the outside corner of the eye (#8).

7. Insert the needle and thread back into the head and pull out at the inside corner of opposite eye (#1). Working on the same side of the face for the rest of this step, go back into the head and down to the outside corner of the lips (#9). Pull out here and then go back inside the head and up to the outside corner of the eye (#10). Insert the needle back into the head, then pull the thread through to the back of the head and anchor it off by taking a couple of small stitches.

Coloring the Head

(figure n)

Colors blend together beautifully on this sample head. This gal is ready to be dressed and have her hair done, which will be explained in the next chapter (page 25).

1. Start the shading using sienna brown or another shade of light brown. Scribble down the temples, around the crease of the upper eyelid (even though it is not there yet), down both sides of the nose, under the nose, around the nose flares, down the center seam under the tip of the nose, under the lower lip, and around the chin area.

2. By shading the face, you are giving it the shadows that imply dimension. With this in mind, you need to decide where your light is coming from so that you know where the shadows will fall. On the side of the face that will have shadows, shade in a bit beyond the chin, going towards the cheek. Shade lightly on the upper lip, around the crease of the smile, and under the lower eyelids. Do not be shy. Really scribble on the color. When it is blended, it fades quite a bit.

3. Next, with a lighter tan, beige, or flesh-colored pencil, start bringing the highlights into the face. Highlights go next to the darker brown, heading toward the higher points of the face. Place the highlights next to the temples, down the sides of the nose, the upper lip, the chin, on the cheekbones under the eyes, and on the brow bone just below the eyebrows.

4. With a white pencil, lighten the center of the forehead the cheekbones under the eyes, and the center of the chin. In these locations, place the white directly on top—and in the center—of the highlights made in the previous step. The white may not be visible on your fabric but it is very important. When blended, you will see how it prevents the other colors from covering that area.

5. With the carmine red, blush the cheek area in exactly the same place you would put blush on a human face. Really layer it on.

6. Wrap a piece of fabric around your index finger and blend all of the colors together.

7. The eyes are next. The doll's eyes are varying shades of one color or three colors. You will need a light, medium, and dark. The eyes for the sample head shown at left (figure n) and in the close-up of the eye opposite (figure o) was colored with light green, grass green, and peacock blue.

8. With the lightest color (light green), fill in the entire iris. On the side of the iris that would be in a shadow, use the middle color (grass green) (figure o). Also apply the middle color underneath the upper eyelid. The darkest color (peacock blue) starts on the inner edge of the upper eyelid and follows the eyelid over to the outer edge. The lower part of the eyelids catches the color from the eyes. Darken the upper part of the iris with this color, touching the upper part of the pupil.

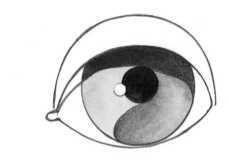

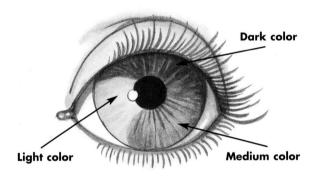

Dark color

Light color

Medium color

(figure o)
Apply color as shown.

9. The lips are shaped using two shades of the color you want. The sample doll uses carmine red for the lighter color and scarlet lake for the darker color. Fill in both the upper and lower lip with the lighter color. Next, using a darker shade, darken the upper lip and the lower part of the lower lip.

10. Using a white pencil, lighten the center of the lower lip.

11. When you have finished the face, seal it with a textile medium and let the face dry for 24 hours. It is best to do this before detailing the face. Otherwise, the pens pick up the pigment from the pencils and get clogged.

12. Using a brown pen, outline the eyelids, draw in the eyelashes, and feather in the eyebrows.

13. With the brown pen, apply a dot for each nostril and then draw half circles on either side of the nose to represent the flares.

14. Outline the lips with a red pen.

15. With a contrasting color of pen, outline the irises and draw in the rods that radiate out from the pupil. The sample head features light green for the overall color, grass green for the medium shading, and peacock blue for the darkest color.

16. Color the pupil with a black pen.

17. Add a dot of white with the white gel pen in the pupil.

18. Seal the face again.

Now your doll is ready to be dressed and have her hair done, which will be explained in the next chapter.

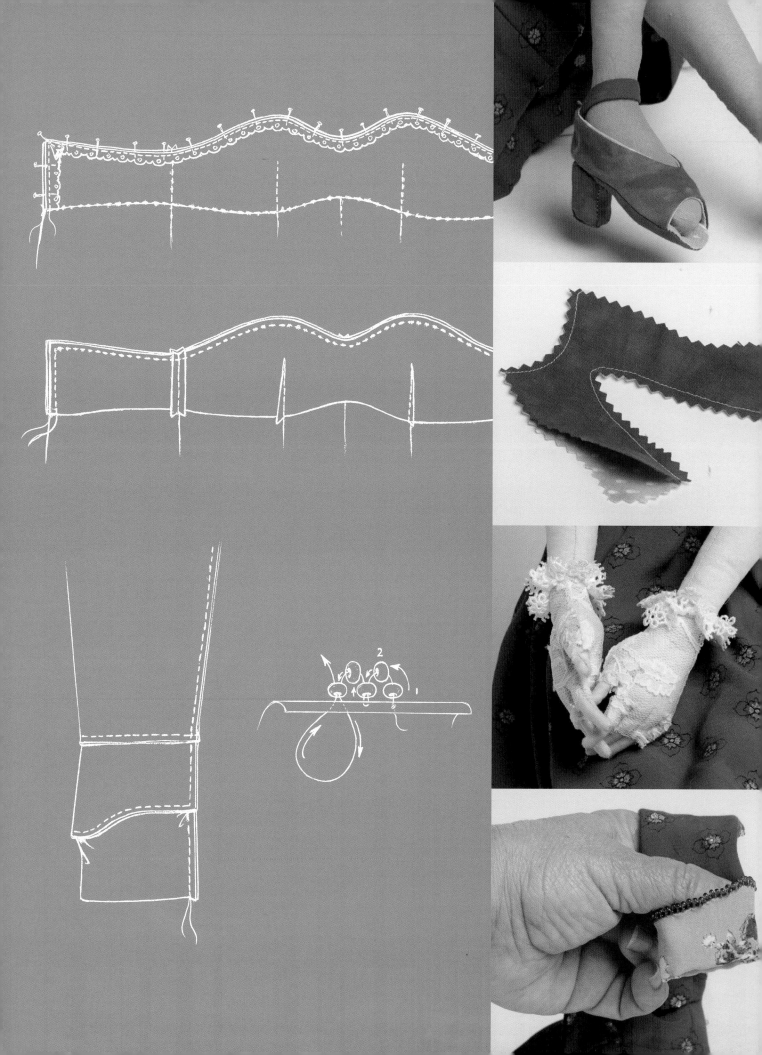

CHAPTER 2

1940S HAUTE COUTURE: FASHIONING A STYLISH SUIT

America lived through enormous challenges in the 1940s. The Greatest Generation went to war overseas. On the home front, women worked in factories to support the fight for freedom. It was a time of great change and sacrifice. Butter, coffee, shoes, and sugar were scarce. So were silk stockings. Uncle Sam asked us to ration our resources, and we did. But along with the limitations came great jazz from the swing orchestras, movie classics such as *Yankee Doodle Dandy* and *Casablanca*, and clothes reflecting the mood portrayed on the silver screen.

By necessity, women went back to the basics. Women of the 1940s wore clothes that reflected a more masculine and square look, hence, the introduction of shoulder pads. Skirts were shorter and more practical. Some designers softened their garments by using rayon fabric. Hats were smaller, but thankfully, bright colors and veils added a touch of glamour. Shoes were open-toed with chunky heels and ankle straps. Purses were square, however, embellishments added a more feminine touch. Women wore their hair longer and more elaborately to compensate for a clothing style that had turned plain Jane.

HELEN

In this chapter, we'll explore efforts in 1944, by some of the New York and Paris designers, to create a more feminine suit design. This suit pairs a traditional square blouse with a shorter pleated skirt. The underwear is soft and feminine. And, with apologies to Uncle Sam, in this book, our gal wears nylon stockings! (In case you were wondering, silk stockings were gone by 1942.)

MATERIALS

basic body (page 10)

¹/₃ yard (30.5 cm) small-print rayon for the jacket and jacket lining

¹/₄ yard (23 cm) small-print rayon for the blouse and jacket cuffs

¹/₄ yard (23 cm) low-loft quilt batting

1 yard (91 cm) pattern drafting paper or tissue paper

¹/₄ yard (23 cm) of silk fabric or a vintage silk scarf or handkerchief for the camiknickers

one half of a pair of nylon knee highs

25" × 18" (63 × 45.7 cm) cotton fabric for the hat, purse, and shoes

scraps of cotton fabric for lining the purse and shoes

9" × 4" (22.9 × 10.2 cm) netting or tulle for the hat

1¹/₂ yards (1.4 m) ¹/₂" (12 mm) -wide lace for the trim on the camiknickers and garters

¹/₄ yard (23 cm) stretch lace for the gloves

1 yard (91 cm) of ¹/₄" (6 mm) -wide lace for the trim on the gloves

¹/₄ yard (23 cm) double sided bonding sheet such as Wonder-Under or Vliesofix

thread to match

14" (35.6 cm) florist wire for the hat brim

black machine sewing thread

beading thread

size 11/12 seed beads in color to match the doll's theme

8 flower-shaped beads for embellishing the garters

2 doll-sized buttons for the camiknickers

8 small buttons: 1 for skirt, 2 for shoes, 5 for blouse

8 small snaps for the blouse, purse, and skirt

hairnet

doll hat-pin

mohair for hair

TOOLS

basic clothing and sewing kits (pages 10–11)

CAMIKNICKERS

Camiknickers were very popular during the early 1940s. Helen's delicate version of the one-piece undergarment was made from an old silk scarf. Garters for the stockings complete the effect.

TIP

Silk can be very tricky to work with. To gain some control over this light, slippery fabric, spray the silk with a liquid stabilizer product called Perfect Sew. Once dry, it gives the fabric a crisp hand so that it cuts and sews like cotton. When your garment is finished, simply rinse it in water to restore the silk to its original drape.

1. Trace all of the camiknicker pattern pieces (pages 110–112) onto tissue paper or pattern drafting paper. Pin the traced shape to the wrong side of the silk scarf or handkerchief that has been doubled, right sides together. The camiknickers Bodice Front is pinned on the fold.

2. Cut out all of the pattern pieces from the fabric using straight-edge fabric scissors.

3. Set aside one Bodice Front and two Bodice Backs for the lining. Work on the remaining bodice pieces as follows: Sew the darts on the front. Pin the side seams of the front to the side seams of the back, right sides together, and sew seam #1 as pinned (figure a).

Note: All camiknicker seam allowances are 1/8" (3 mm) unless otherwise noted.

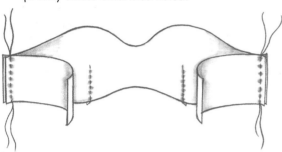

(figure a)
Assemble the bodice.

4. Dart and join the remaining bodice front and backs, following the same instructions in step 2, above, to make the lining. Set the assembled piece aside.

5. With right sides of the Center Front fabric pieces together, sew seam #2.

6. Pin one side of a Center Front to a Side Front, right sides together, at seam #3, and sew (figure b). Attach the remaining Side Front to the other side.

(figure b)
Attach the Side Fronts to the Center Front.

7. Sew the darts in the Center Back fabric pieces, then sew the 2 pieces together at seam #4, right sides together, leaving open where marked. Do not sew the crotch.

8. Pin the joined backs to the fronts, right sides together, and sew down the sides along seams #5 (figure c).

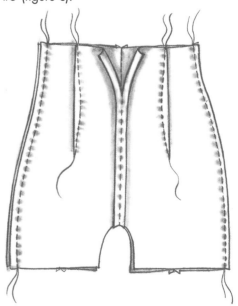

(figure c)
Join the front to the back at the sides.

9. With right sides together, pin the lower part of the camiknickers (the joined back and front) to the bodice at seam #6, and then sew from one opening to the other side around the bodice.

10. Pin the small lace to the bodice at the top starting along the center back edge, with the bottom edge of the trim aligned with the top edge of the bodice, right sides together (figure d). Sew in place.

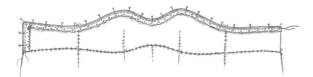

(figure d)
The lace is at the top of the bodice when the lining is sewn and turned.

11. Pin the bodice lining to the bodice, right sides together, and sew across the top and down both sides at the back, catching the edge of the lace between the seam allowances (figure e). Turn the bodice lining to the inside of the garment. With needle and thread, hand sew the lining to the inside of the bodice, turning under a small hem

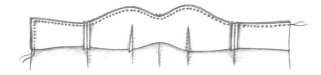

as you sew.

(figure e)
Attach the lace and join the lining.

12. Fold up a 1/8" (3 mm) deep hem along the legs of the camiknickers. Baste in place. Pin the small lace to the right side of the hem, on the outside of the hem. Sew the lace in place.

13. Pin the front and back along the crotch, right sides together. Sew from one hemline of a leg opening to the other side (figure f).

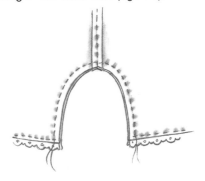

(figure f)
Seam the crotch after the legs are hemmed.

14. Hand sew snaps to the opening at the top of the camiknickers Bodice Back on the outside on one side, and on the inside of the other side. Sew one just below the top edge and another one just above the seam where the bodice meets the lower part of the knickers. On the outside, sew small buttons at the snap locations.

15. Measure more of the small lace for the straps and hand sew them in place, as marked on the Bodice Front pieces. Slip the camiknickers on the doll and mark the placement of the straps on the back of the bodice. Remove the camiknickers from the doll and hand sew the straps where marked.

16. Cut four 1" (2.5 cm) lengths of the small lace for garters. Hand sew these at the front and back of the legs to represent the garters.

17. Take one stocking from a pair of nylon knee highs, and turn it wrong side out.

18. Machine sew, using a stretch stitch and black thread, from the bottom of the stocking up to the top, on one side. Repeat on the other side of the same stocking. This will create two doll stockings.

19. Cut out the stockings close to your stitching, turn them right side out, and slip them on the doll's legs. Hand sew the garters to the top of the stockings. Use a flower-shaped bead at each stitching point to add a nice embellishment.

Using black thread in the sewing machine when sewing the stockings creates the effect of dark back seams that were popular during this era.

The Blouse

1. Trace all of the Blouse pattern pieces (pages 110, 114) onto tissue paper or pattern drafting paper. Pin them to the wrong side of the blouse fabric of choice that has been doubled, right sides together. Cut two Blouse Backs and one Blouse Front. The Blouse Front is cut on the fabric fold.

2. Mark and sew the darts on the Blouse Front. Pin in the pleat on the Blouse Front, and on the right side of the fabric sew down the entire pleat line.

Before sewing up the side seams of the Blouse, it is best to insert the sleeves.

3. Fold over the pleat to the left of the Blouse Front. Pin it in place.

4. With right sides together, sew the Blouse Front to the Blouse Back at seam #7, the shoulders.

5. Cut out one Blouse Front Lining and one Blouse Back Lining, on the fabric fold. Sew the front and back lining pieces at the shoulders, right sides together.

6. Pin the lining to the blouse, right sides together, and sew along the neck, starting at the opening in the back. Clip the curves of the lining, or trim the seam allowances with pinking shears (figure g).

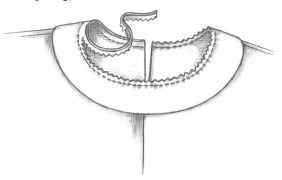

(figure g)
Join the front and back lining at the shoulders, then seam to the blouse neckline.

7. Cut out two Sleeve pattern pieces, and machine sew a running stitch for gathering along the cap of the sleeves as marked.

8. Pull these gathering stitches to fit into the sleeve opening on the blouse. Pin the sleeve in place, and sew it into the arm opening, right sides together.

9. With right sides together, machine sew from the bottom of the sleeves down to the bottom of the blouse along Seam #7 (figure h).

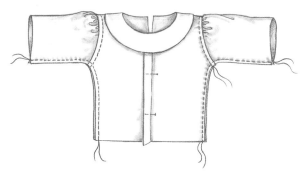

(figure h)
Insert the sleeves before stitching the side seams.

10. To flatten the neck lining, fold it inside the garment and then hand sew it to the inside of the blouse by just tacking it to the shoulder seams and to the pleat on the blouse front.

11. Hand or machine sew a hem in the sleeves and the bottom of the blouse.

12. Turn under a ⅛" (3 mm) hem at the center back openings and machine sew. Hand sew snaps on the blouse opening in the back, and hand sew five small buttons down the front of the blouse.

THE SKIRT

1. Cut three fabric panels for the skirt, each measuring 9" long by 7½" wide (22.9 × 19 cm).

2. Cut out the waistband using the pattern (page 110). Sew the waistband by folding it in half lengthwise, right sides together, and sewing across each of the ends (figure i).

(figure i)
Fold the waistband lengthwise and stitch across both of the short ends.

3. Sew the three skirt panels together, right sides together, along the short ends.

4. Measure out evenly distributed pleats in the skirt using the waistband as your guide, and pin in the pleats. Iron the pleats flat.

5. With right sides together, pin the skirt to one side of the waistband, right sides together, and machine sew it in place (figure j).

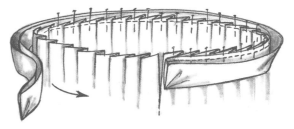

(figure j)
Sew the waistband to the pleated skirt.

6. Fold down the top half of the waistband to the inside of the skirt and hand sew it along the inner edge.

7. Sew the back seam of the skirt, right sides together, leaving a 1½" (3.8 cm) opening below the waistband. Turn under a ⅛" (3 mm) seam allowance and hand sew it flat.

8. Fold the skirt hem in place, iron, and then hand sew the hem. Sew a snap on the waistband at the overlapped opening and add a button on the outside of the waistband (figure k).

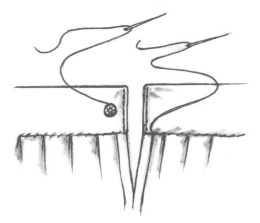

(figure k)
Hand sew the long, loose edge of the waistband inside the skirt.

THE JACKET

1. Trace all of the jacket pattern pieces (pages 110–113) on to tissue paper or pattern drafting paper. Cut out all of the fabric pieces from the jacket fabric and lining. Use pinking shears if you are using rayon to help prevent fraying.

2. Machine gather the Jacket Upper Bodice, as marked along the bottom edge.

3. With right sides together, and matching seam #8, sew the Jacket Lower Front to the Jacket Upper Bodice (figure l).

Note: All jacket seam allowances are 1/8" (3 mm) unless otherwise noted.

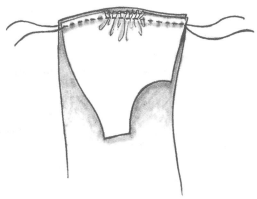

(figure l)
Gather the Upper Bodice at the bustline before seaming to the Lower Front.

4. With right sides together, sew the Jacket Back pieces along seam #2.

5. Pin the jacket back to the jacket fronts at the shoulders, right sides together, and sew (figure m).

6. Sew the back to the fronts at the side, seam #10, at this time, right sides together (figure m). Unlike the blouse, the sleeves will be inserted later because the jacket has a lining.

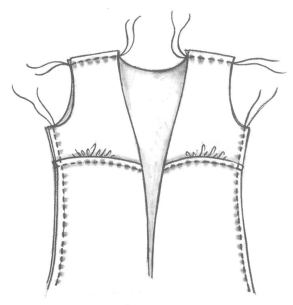

(figure m)
Seam the Fronts to the Back at the shoulders and sides.

7. Following steps 2–6, sew the lining pieces as you did the outside of the jacket.

8. Before sewing the lining to the main jacket, cut the ties. The ties are cut from the same fabric as the jacket. They measure 5 1/2" long by 1 1/4" wide (14 × 3.2 cm). Fold each one in half, right sides together, and sew from one end, down the length of the tie, and leaving open at the other end. Turn them right sides out, using tubes or straws. Iron flat.

9. Pin the tie where marked on the right side of both jacket fronts, with the unstitched edges in the seam allowances and the rest of the ties loose against the right side of the body.

10. With right sides together, pin the lining to the jacket body along the front edges and neckline.

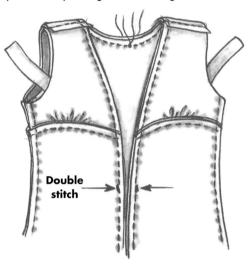

(figure n)
Prepare the lining and attach it to the body.

11. Starting at the back of the neck, sew all the way around the outer seams (figure n). Double stitch where the ties are pinned.

To make sure the ties don't catch in the seam lines, pull them through the sleeve openings.

12. Trim with pinking shears, leaving a scant 1/8" (3 mm) seam allowance. Turn the body and lining right side out. Iron all of the seams flat.

13. With the mechanical pencil, trace two cuffs onto the wrong side of the blouse fabric. Do not cut out the shapes yet. Double the fabric, right sides together, and sew across the top of the cuff. Cut out the shapes, turn each one right side out along the seam line, and iron them flat (figure o).

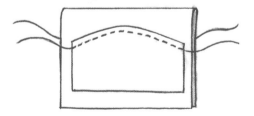

(figure o)
Sew, then cut out the cuffs from the blouse fabric.

14. Machine sew the cuffs at the wrists of the jacket sleeves, right sides together (figure p). Sew just one side of the cuff.

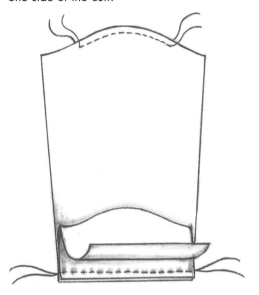

(figure p)
Attach the cuff to the bottom of each sleeve.

15. Sew a gathering stitch at the cap of each sleeve. With right sides together, sew each of the sleeves together along the underarm seam. It helps to open up the cuffs and sew from the top of the sleeve all the way down to the end of the opened-up cuff (figure q).

(figure q)
Sew the underarm seam.

16. Fold back the top half of the cuff, and hand sew it to the inside of the sleeve.

17. Insert the sleeves into the jacket armhole, right sides together. Pin them in place and machine sew the sleeves into the jacket.

> Setting in the sleeves is the trickiest part of making this outfit. It is kind of challenging, but using a ¼" (6 mm) presser foot on your machine really helps. If you do not have this presser foot, use the smallest foot available.

18. Iron the jacket again and it is finished!

Hand-sewn size 11/12 seed beads at the center of the flower design on the jacket add just the right amount of embellishment. This is a delightful technique and is so easy.

THE CUFF-BEADED EDGING

1. Thread up a beading needle with 2 yards (1.8 m) of beading thread, and place a knot in one end.

2. Anchor the thread on the underside of the cuff with a few small stitches and then come out at the top edge.

3. Add three seed beads to the needle and thread. Go back into the cuff next to where the needle and thread first came out. You now have a picot.

4. Taking a tiny stitch, come out the edge of the cuff beside the last bead you added and pull through the hole in that bead (figure r).

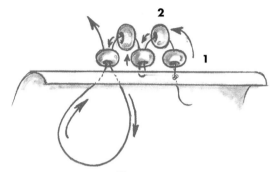

(figure r)
Hand-stitch the picot edging to each cuff.

5. Add two new beads to the needle and thread and pull through the edge of the cuff next to the bead that you just pulled through.

6. Repeat steps 4 and 5 until you have edged the entire cuff with picots. Anchor the thread with a few small stitches and cut it off.

THE GLOVES

In the 1940s and '50s, women did not go anywhere without gloves. In the summer, they generally wore lightweight, lacey, or half-glove versions. Your doll has two fingers that are not separate, so half-gloves are easier to make.

1. Trace two glove patterns (page 113) onto tissue paper or pattern drafting paper.

2. Pin the traced pattern pieces onto the wrong side of doubled stretch lace fabric.

3. Sew along the tracing and sewing lines as shown on the pattern pieces, leaving open at the wrist where marked. Cut out the stitched shapes with straight-edge fabric scissors, using ⅛" (3 mm) seam allowances. Tear away the paper (figure s). Turn each glove right side out, and slip them onto the doll's hands.

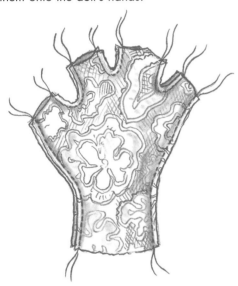

(figure s)
Sew the gloves with the paper tracing in place.

4. With a needle and thread, hand sew the trim along the wrist edge of the gloves. Tuck in the raw edges of the lace around the doll's fingers.

Delicate lace gloves stitch up with ease when a paper tracing of the pattern piece is used as a stabilizer while stitching.

THE SHOES

1. Trace two Shoe Top pattern pieces (page 112) onto the wrong side of the fabric.

2. Pin a Shoe Top to the (uncut) lining fabric, right sides together, and sew along both of the tracing and sewing lines, at the top edge and the toes. Cut out the lining with pinking shears and turn the piece right side out (figure t). Make the second lined top in the same manner.

Note: all seam allowances are 1/8" (3 mm) wide unless otherwise noted.

(figure t)
Sew the toe and the top opening to the lining fabric before cutting out the lining.

3. Open up the back so that the lining and fabrics match and, with right sides together, sew this opening closed (figure u).

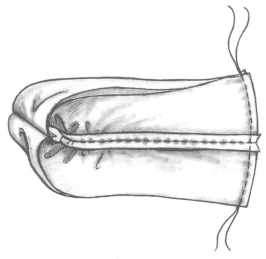

(figure u)
Join the Shoe Top and the lining along the back seams.

4. Fold the lining to the inside and iron.

5. Cut out two Shoe Soles pattern pieces (page 114) from the fabric and two from the lining fabric. If necessary, trim the lower raw edges of the lining to the same length as the outer shoe. First, though, make sure that the seam lines for the toe and foot openings are at the edges.

6. On both of the lining pieces, cut a 1" (2.5 cm) long slit down the center. Set aside one shoe and continue with the following steps.

7. With right sides together, pin the bottom edge of the shoe top to the Shoe Sole. Starting at one side of the toe opening, sew around the outer edge.

8. Pin a lining to the Shoe Top with right side of the sole lining to the wrong side of the Shoe Top (figure v). Sew all the way around the outer edge.

(figure v)
Sandwich the Shoe Top and lining inside the sole pieces.

9. Clip through the seam allowances along the curves and then turn the shoe right side out through the slit in the lining. Make sure that the shoe top is turned right side out.

10. Cut out the Cardboard Sole Insert (page 113) and slip it into the shoe through the opening in the lining. This insert gives the bottom of the shoe stability. Repeat steps 7–9 for the remaining shoe.

11. Cut out all the heel patterns (page 112). You need four Heel Sides, two Heel Fronts, two Heel Backs, and two Heel Bottoms.

12. With right sides together, pin one Heel Side to one Heel Front, and sew down the length of seam #9. Join another Heel Side to the same Heel Front at the remaining seam #9.

13. Pin the Heel Back to the two Heel Sides, right sides together, and sew down each seam #10. You now have a square-looking shape.

14. Pin the Heel Bottom to the lower edges of the heel that you just created, right sides together.

15. Sew the Heel Back to the Heel Bottom along seam #11, as pinned. At the corner of the Heel bottom, make sure that the previously stitched vertical seam (#10) is caught in the stitching. Leave the needle down in the fabric. Lift the presser foot, pivot the heel pieces, and lower the presser foot so that you can sew seam #12, which joins the Heel Bottom to the Heel Side. Continue stitching around the pinned heel pieces, pivoting at the corners and catching the bottoms of each vertical seam (figure w). At the end of the current seam, you will be catching the bottom of vertical seam (#9). Then you will sew seam #13 to join the Heel Bottom to the Heel Front. The last edges to be joined are a Heel Bottom to a Heel Side, with another seam #12.

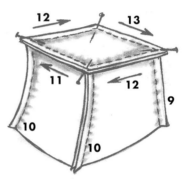

(figure w)
Join the Heel Front, Back, and Sides before adding the Heel Bottom.

16. Turn the heel right side out, and fill it with stuffing. Pin the heel to the bottom of the shoe and hand sew it in place (figure x).

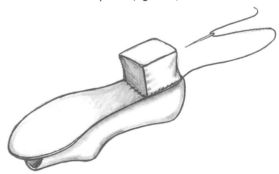

(figure x)
Hand sew the stuffed heel to the bottom of the shoe.

17. Cut a 3" × ³⁄₄" (7.6 × 1.9 cm) -wide piece of fabric on the bias for the ankle strap. Fold the strap in half lengthwise, right sides together, and sew down the length of the strap, using a scant ¹⁄₈" (3 mm) seam allowance. Sew one end closed. Turn, using a turning tool.

18. Measure the length of strap needed to wrap around the ankle and attach to the back of the shoe. Cut the raw end of the strap to fit. Hand sew the raw end to the inside of the shoe back. Slip the shoe on the doll's foot, wrap the strap around her ankle, and pin it toward the back.

19. Hand sew the strap to the shoe and add a button (figure y).

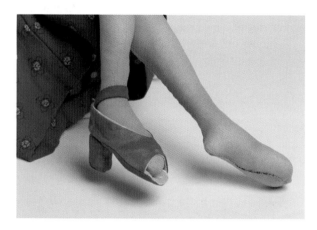

(figure y)
The ankle strap secures the shoe permanently to the doll's foot.

THE HAT

1. Trace all of the pattern pieces (pages 110; 113, 114) onto the paper side of a double-sided bonding sheet such as Pellon Wonder Under or Vlisofix. Iron the bonding sheet onto the wrong side of the hat fabric. Cut out all of the pieces and peel off the paper backing. Be sure to cut out the hole for the center of the Hat Brim.

2. Lay the fabric Hat Brim on the right side of the fabric and cut out another Brim for the lining.

3. Using an iron, fuse the wrong side of the Hat Top, Hat Side, and Hat Brim cut from hat fabric (not lining) onto a piece of quilt batting. Cut out the shapes.

4. With right sides together, sew the back seam of the Hat Side.

5. Pin the Hat Top to the Hat Side, right sides together, and sew along the edge (figure z).

(figure z)
Seam together the Hat Top and Hat Side.

6. Pin the inner edge of the Hat Brim to the bottom of the Hat Side, right sides together, and sew (figure z).

7. Pin the Hat Brim lining to the Hat, right sides together, and sew along the outer edge (figure aa).

(figure aa)
Seam together the Hat Brim pieces.

8. Clip through the seam allowances of all curved seams. Turn the hat, right sides out, and iron it flat. Measure a piece of wire to fit around the outer edge inside the brim of the hat, and secure it in a circle. Insert the wire and machine sew along brim, just inside of the wire, to keep it in place.

9. On the inside of the brim, hand sew the inner edge of the Hat Brim lining to the Hat Side, for a finished look.

10. Arrange the netting or tulle on the top of the hat. Hand sew it in place.

The Hair

1. Hand sew the mohair in place in clumps around the head of the doll. Each clump of mohair is spaced 3/4" (1.9 cm) apart. Follow the seam of the head as you hand sew it to the head. Catch each clump in its center with the thread. This secures it to the head. Fluff it up with your fingers. If you need more at the center of the head add a couple more clumps.

2. Cut a small piece of the hair net and tie the raw ends in a knot. Slip this over the doll's hair and secure it to the head using a needle and thread (figure ab).

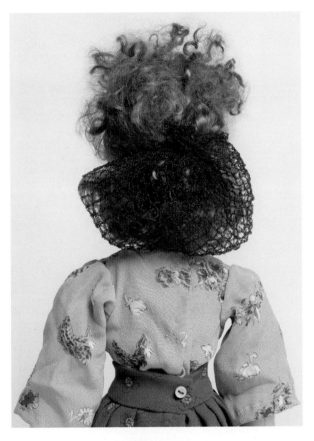

(figure ab)
Sew on clumps of mohair and cover the back with a hair net.

3. Secure the hat to the doll's head with a hat pin. *Note: The pretty fabric flower on her hat is explained on pages 90–91.*

The Purse

1. Trace the Clutch Purse template (page 114) onto the wrong side of a piece of lining fabric. Pin this piece to the purse fabric, right sides together. Pin a piece of thin quilt batting against the wrong side of the fabric.

2. Sew around the outer edges, leaving open where marked. Cut out all of the joined layers with pinking shears, and turn the purse right side out through the opening so that the batting is in the middle. Iron flat.

3. Machine sew the opening closed.

4. Fold the clutch at the first fold line, right sides together. Sew both side seams through all layers (figure ac). Be sure to back stitch at the top edge of each seam. Turn the clutch right side out.

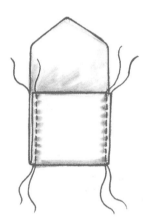

(figure ac)
Sew the sides of the purse.

5. Fold down the clutch flap along the second fold line. Sew a fabric flower (page 90–91) to the outside. Sew a snap inside of the flap. Sew the other side of the snap on the body of the purse. You now have a clutch purse for your doll to carry all her treasures.

Congratulations! You have made it through a chapter with a ton of information. You learned basic sewing techniques and are now ready to get adventurous. Warm up your imagination—in the next chapters you will have fun with nontraditional techniques for clothing design.

GALLERY

MARION

Marion Bolson

The artist writes:

The inspiration for this ensemble came from a vintage McCall's pattern dated January 1940. The pattern is printed with this line: "Insist on a McCall pattern, it's the short cut to Paris style." I really wanted to create something elegant with beading and this design seemed the perfect canvas. The suit is made from a lush brown silk dupioni. It is embellished with size 13 charlotte beads in dark brown, olive green, black, and gold. The shoes and purse are in the same silk with beading. The black gloves are made from two-way spandex with beaded hems. The fur muff and hat are made from the fur cuff off an old coat. Her jewelry is made from crystal gold-lined faceted beads and gold-colored round beads.

The blouse pattern is cut down and has additional darts in the front and back to create the flare for the suit bodice. The straight skirt with darts in the front and back had to be drafted by draping paper towels on the figure and transferring marks where the sewing lines should be. The suit top and skirt patterns were both tested in paper towels first and then in muslin before I started working with the silk.

ODE TO CAROLE LOMBARD

Camille CS Pratt

The artist writes:

The film star Carole Lombard was the personification of glamour for me and the inspiration for this doll. She had a bright spirit, a sincere charm, a sharp sense of humor, and a sparkling presence, to boot.

With this image in mind, I began to research her clothing. I wanted something that embodied all I sensed from Carole and the time she lived in. I found it in a photo of a 1930s-era wedding dress. I wanted to take the simple lines of that dress, add a twist of Hollywood in its heyday, and transform it into something Carole would have been proud to be seen in. Out came paper and pencil, silks and beads, Swarovski crystals, and my imagination. The outcome was a costume I took great pleasure in designing and bringing to fruition.

The doll has elegant sheer silk stockings attached to the garters of a beautiful dupioni silk girdle. Her underbodice is dupioni silk, hand beaded for texture. The overbodice is an antique piece of overdyed silk. Complementing the bodice is a skirt of crepe-backed satin in a rich shade of eggplant with beaded hem and graceful train.

She carries a small silk box purse from the same era, complete with a mirrored lid and beaded handle. A pair of crepe satin gloves add a touch of elegance. She is properly and tastefully bejeweled with crystals right down to her shoes.

KATHRYN

Antonette Cely

The artist writes:

What I like most about the fashion of the 1940s is the combination of tailored clothes with feminine frills. It was also an era when women were just beginning to wear pants outside the bedroom. I focused mainly on Katharine Hepburn as my inspiration. She championed women wearing pants in the '30s and '40s and still looked feminine while doing so.

I used a textured woven striped fabric for her suit, and found some lovely pleated cotton lawn for her collar and cuffs. I built shoulder pads right into her shoulders so the suit would have that broad-shouldered look that is so prevalent in this period. The shoes are suede high-heeled loafers, with a matching suede handbag.

I love the fact that this doll pattern has feminine curves, creating a very female silhouette even though she is wearing a tailored suit. The shoes were the most fun, though, and I used the same method I always use for making shoes. I made polymer clay shoe lasts and then constructed the shoes right onto those hard forms. The structure is formed from manila file folders. Suede is glued directly onto the surface. These shoes don't have a stitch of thread in them, except for the traditional hand stitching at the sides of the uppers. That was very freeing for me, since I'm always distracted by making the sewing match.

I decided not to give this doll a hat, because I love the big, exaggerated hairdos of the 1940s and didn't want to hide hers.

GALLERY

43

ჿEANNE ᲧICHELLE

Betts Vidal

The artist writes:

For inspiration, I decided to once again view my video of *The Women* starring Joan Crawford, Norma Shearer, and Rosalind Russell. It's filmed in black and white with a midmovie fashion show in *Wizard of Oz*–like color.

In an old *Smithsonian* magazine, I found a black-and-white photo titled "Dazzle by the Dozen" by Irving Penn that featured twelve top fashion models of 1947 posed in evening gowns. How elegant!

I had found my inspiration. My doll would wear black and white. I would use a bias cut, diagonal detail, movie star drama, diamonds, opera gloves, a veiled hat, and a photo-shoot pose.

Two triangles and a 20" (51 cm) circle of fine tricot formed her gown. Satin bias trim swirled into a diagonal detail. Ninety inches of gathered pinstripe taffeta finished the evening ensemble.

Fifty or sixty Austrian crystals strategically glued became earrings, a choker, and bracelets. Opera gloves? I just used glove fabric for arms and hands. For her hat, I covered a 4" (10 cm) cardboard circle with tricot and added a bunched-up vintage veil. The net was in very poor condition but looked sassy when bunched.

Donna Karan says comfy shoes are appropriate any-where, anytime. I agree. Laboriously, I formed scal-loped velvet trim into DK-style shoes. They are hidden beneath the gown, as they should be.

⑤EULAH

Drusilla Esslinger

The artist writes:

One of my favorite people while growing up in the 1940s was our neighbor, Beulah. Beulah had a lot of patience with me as she helped teach me to sew in 1946. This doll is inspired by her and how she dressed.

The doll is made from one of Patti's patterns with slight adjustments. The mature body was made in one piece. The arm is one piece with a thumb added to hold her pocketbook and handkerchief. The foot was made slimmer so she could wear the smaller shoes I made. The head was not changed.

Underneath, she's wearing a teddie, a piece of lingerie my mother always wore, a slip and hose with a seam up the back.

When I am designing, I go to my pattern file, choose the style, and adjust the pattern to the doll. This doll needed a pleated skirt so she can sit down with ease. I altered Patti's pattern for this, choosing silk for the fabric even though linen, rayon, or wool were more commonly used in this period. This lighter fabric is more manageable and gives a similar look. A princess-style jacket allows for more ease.

Her hat, worn cocked to the side with her pageboy hairstyle, is made in two pieces from felt with a feather added for flair. Gloves are made from the same pattern as the hand. Her leather pocketbook, belt, and shoes complete the look of 1946!

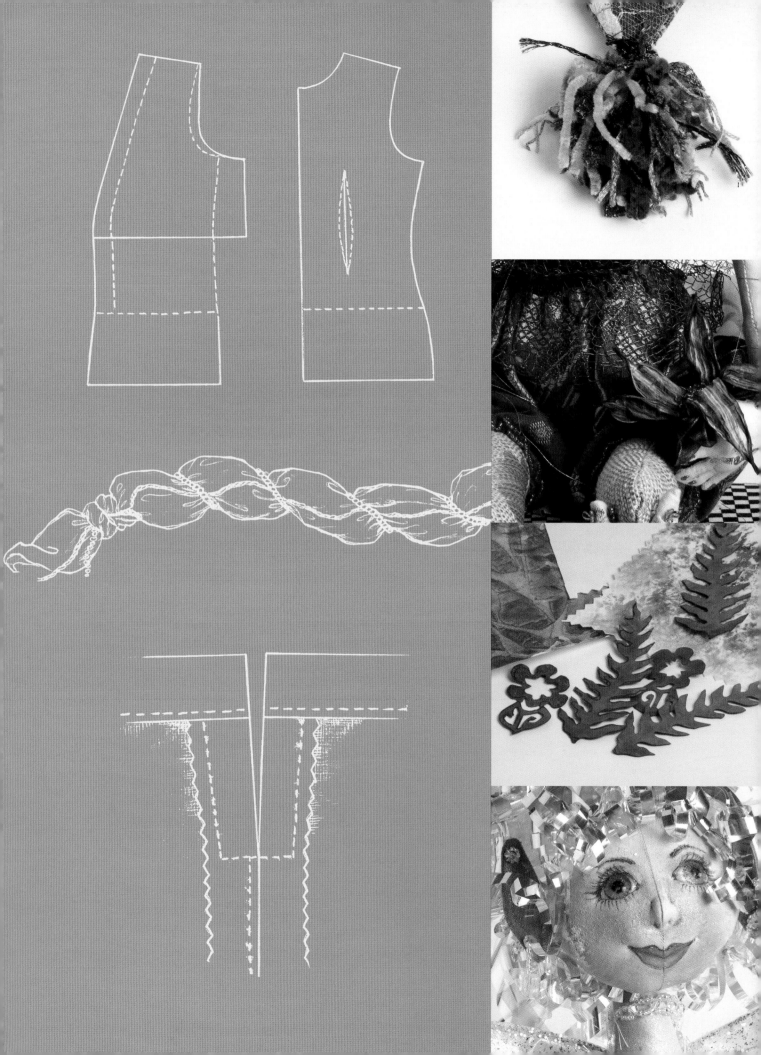

CHAPTER 3

1960S COLLAGE: LAYERING APPLIQUÉS, FIBER, AND TRANSFERS

As it turned out, we needed more than love to get through this period of American history. What memories! Do you have visions of hippies with layers of clothing made from natural fibers dancing to the music of the Beatles, the Rolling Stones, the Supremes, and Otis Redding? There were the Mods and the Rockers with their miniskirts and velvet with loads of fringe. Men in bell-bottoms started wearing jewelry and women's hair ran the gamut from short, stylized, Vidal Sassoon cuts to elaborate coifs, piled high.

Designers such as Betsey Johnson, Zandra Rhodes, Mary Quant, and Tiger Morse introduced a full range of fashion, from soft, flowing, feminine clothing to the straight lines of a miniskirt. Twiggy, Jean Shrimpton, Lauren Hutton, and Veruschka showed us how to wear these styles. From the elegant Jacqueline Kennedy to frumpy Janis Joplin, we saw the entire spectrum of fashion. The love-ins of Haight-Ashbury, mixed-media discotheques of Manhattan, battlefields of Vietnam, and the troubled streets of big-city America all influenced what was designed and worn. Styles in clothing swept the country and then, often without any reason, dropped from what was "in" faster than a one-hit pop star. Clothing was often used as a signature, defining who we were, what we thought, what we liked, and what we hated.

ELIZABETHE

In this chapter, existing pattern pieces are used to create a mixture of mod, hippie, and high-fashion clothing; it will be a collage of styles made with collage techniques.

MATERIALS

basic body pattern pieces, with jointed or straight legs, as desired (pages 107–109)

1/4 yard (23 cm) flesh-colored batik cotton for doll body

1/4 yard (23 cm) purple batik cotton for skirt edging

1/4 yard (23 cm) polka-dot cotton fabric for legs

12" (30.5 cm) square red cotton for shoes

1/4 yard (23 cm) silk chiffon or silk chiffon scarf

1/4 yard (23 cm) white or cream-colored silky polyester fabric for skirt

1/4 yard (23 cm) tulle or fine netting in cream or color to match your theme

1 yard (91 cm) of 5" (12.7 cm) -wide lace for skirt

1 yard (91 cm) of 1/3" (1 cm) -wide trim for skirt

32" (81.3 cm) of 1/4" (6 mm) -wide ribbon for boot laces

20" (50.8 cm) yarn for headband, such as Knitting Fever Macao ribbon yarn

scraps of lace, metallic threads, ribbons, and yarns for collage

snippets of brocade, metallic, silk fabrics for collage

2 yards (1.8 m) of two different yarns for purse strap and tassel

Meadowbrook Industries Angelina Heat-Bondable Fiber (Hot Fix) in colors to match your theme. (*Note: Make sure you use the Meadowbrook product, as there is another version. Angelina is sold through Textura Trading [see Resources, page 120] or at local quilt and yarn shops.*)

decorative machine threads

threads to match

1 snap for skirt

1 small button for skirt

2 sheets Jacquard Inkjet Print on Silk

heat-transfer inks or paints

image to print on silk

size 11/12 seed beads in 5 colors

size 6/7 seed beads that coordinate with the size 11/12 seed beads

accent beads to match your color theme

beading thread

costume jewelry

colored pencils

white gel pen

Zig Millennium or Micron Pigma pens: black, brown, red

Mohair or Tibetan goat hair

4 sheets white printer or copy paper

small sea sponges, one for each color

1 sheet cardstock paper

2 sheets of baking parchment paper

double-sided, iron-on, water-soluble stabilizer such as Floriani Wet N Gone Fusible Dissolvable Stabilizer, Freudenberg Solusheet/Vilene 541, Mokuba Free Lace, Brother/Foundation Aqua-Melt Water-Soluble Stabilizer

TOOLS

basic body, clothing, fabric-dyeing, and sewing kits (pages 10–11)

free-motion or darning presser foot

size 12 topstitch or embroidery sewing machine needle

The Body and Fabric Collage Bodice

The Bodice (or blouse) is made from fabric created using collage techniques. You are creating your own fabric to use for the bodice. This Bodice includes her upper body and arms. Instead of making separate clothing, the decorated cloth is used to make several body parts.

1. Before the body of the doll is made, the collage work needs to be done. Collect the materials for this and clear a space on a table. You will need the flesh-colored batik fabric, silk chiffon or silk scarf, and all your bits and pieces of brocade, lace, fabrics and threads, silk fabric, and yarns, as well as the tulle or fine netting.

2. Place several colors of Angelina between two protective sheets of parchment paper. Set iron at a medium temperature and press for about three seconds. If you overheat the Angelina, it will lose its sheen. Let the sheets cool, then remove the Angelina fiber.

3. Choose the silk chiffon or silk scarf to be encrusted with embellishments. Tear the Angelina into smaller pieces and place them onto half of the silk surface, then throw down snippets of fabrics, threads, and yarns. You will want a scattering of snippets. Allow the Angelina fibers to show. On top of this, lay the other half of the silk. Pin through all layers in several places.

4. With decorative thread in the upper threader of your sewing machine, and any thread in the bobbin, free-motion sew all over the layered items. (See the tip on page 90 for more guidance on free-motion embroidery stitching.) Be sure to sew the lines of stitching closely together, as you will be cutting out pieces of this fabric for parts of the body.

5. Cut the flesh-colored batik fabric in half. On the wrong side of one piece, trace the Face, Hand, Head Back, and Upper Body Front pattern pieces. On the other piece of fabric, trace the Arm, Body Back, and Lower Body Front. Cut the Upper Body Front from the batik fabric. Sew, then cut out and finish assembling, the Hands and head. (See steps 1–5 and 12–15, on pages 13 and 15–16).

6. Iron the double-sided, iron-on stabilizer to the wrong side of your collage fabric. Peel off the paper backing.

7. Lay the collage fabric, bonded side down, on the right side of the batik fabric where the arms and remaining body pieces are traced. Iron it in place. Cut out all but the arms. Fold the fabric in half where the arms are traced and sew, then cut them out (figure a) (step 11, page 15).

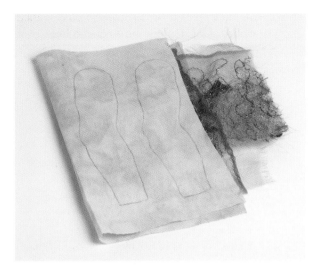

(figure a)
Overlay the collage fabric on the batik fabric.

8. Following the instructions for sewing the body in Chapter 1, page 18, sew the body pieces, including joining the Upper Body Front to the Lower Body Front.

9. The legs are traced and sewn using the polka-dot fabric following the sewing instructions in Chapter 1 for jointed legs (page 16) or straight legs (page 17). Fill all of the body parts with stuffing and sew them together.

10. Following the beaded-edge illustration and instructions (page 34), and using the size 11/12 seed beads, bead the collage-fabric bodice of the Body Front. Bead the seams where the hands were sewn to the arms.

THE SKIRT

1. Gather the inks or paints, sponges, patterns for the leaf and flower designs (page 115), card-stock paper and the printer or copy paper. Trace the leaf and flower onto the cardstock and cut them out using paper scissors.

TIP

Heat-transfer inks or paints are used mainly for coloring polyester fabrics. They do not transfer well onto natural fibers. They are a wonderful way of coloring fabric and they leave the hand (personality when draped) of the fabric very soft and natural. Because theses paints are heated to transfer the colors, this single step also permanently sets the colors.

2. Pour the inks or paints onto a piece of cardstock. Using the sponges, pick up the inks and dab them onto the copy paper. Place the templates down, one at a time, and dab onto them. Remove the templates and set them down in another area of the copy paper. This gives you shadow images (figure b). The colors used on the sample doll were yellow, bottle green, ultramarine, and claret.

(figure b)
Paint on paper.

3. Let the papers dry completely and then place them, colored side down, onto the right side of the silky polyester fabric, which is cut into a 7" × 24" piece (17.8 × 61 cm).

> Does polyester have a right or wrong side? It is hard to tell. Look at the selvedge (the edges). You will see little holes where the fabric was attached to the loom. The holes will feel smooth on the right side of the fabric, whereas the wrong side will feel bumpy at those spots.

4. Place a protective sheet on your ironing board. Place the fabric on the protective sheet and, on top of the fabric, the paper. Set the iron at the hottest setting and iron, holding it in place for about 8 seconds. Lift up a corner of the paper to see if the color has transferred to the fabric. If not, hold the iron in place a bit longer.

5. Because the templates of the leaves and flowers were painted, their images can be transferred to the fabric. Place them, colored side down, onto the right side of the fabric and iron them to transfer the images. Cover them with a protective sheet before ironing. This adds a positive image to the fabric.

6. Copy the image desired for the skirt onto the inkjet-silk. Peel the paper backing from the silk and iron double-sided iron-on stabilizer to the back of the silk.

> The sample doll used a drawing I did. I scanned the drawing and placed it into Adobe Photoshop. I then made a picture package with four images on a page, which reduced the drawing to the proper size for the skirt. I printed two of these images onto the silk. If you want to use my drawing it is included on page 115.

7. Cut out the images and iron them along the bottom of the polyester fabric. Machine sew with decorative thread in the needle around the images. Any thread can be in the bobbin as it will not show. You can free-motion or straight stitch around the images.

8. To take up some of the bulk along the waistline, sew seven darts along the top (24" or 61 cm) edge of the fabric (figure c). Each dart should be ⅛" (3 mm) deep and approximately 3¼" (8.3 cm) apart.

(figure c)
Sew seven darts in the skirt waist.

9. With a straight stitch set for a gathering stitch length, machine sew along the top edge of the skirt.

10. Following steps 2, 4, 5, and 6 of the skirt assembly instructions in Chapter 2 (page 31) cut out and sew the waistband, and attach the skirt to the waistband.

11. Trace the Skirt Edging pattern onto the wrong side of the fabric chosen for this, which has been cut 9" × 24" (22.9 × 61 cm). Use a colored pencil so you can see your traced lines. You will need to move the edging pattern piece as you trace it along the top edge of the fabric. Fold the fabric in half widthwise (fold so that the edging is finished on both sides), right sides together. Machine sew along the traced lines. Cut out the stitched shape with pinking shears and using ⅛" (3 mm) seam allowances. Turn the edging right side out and iron it flat.

12. With right sides together and raw edges even, pin the Skirt Edging to the bottom of the skirt. On top of the edging, place the 5" (12.7 cm) -wide lace. Machine sew the layers in place. Turn down the edging and lace and iron flat.

13. Collect the narrow trim and pin it along the seam where the Skirt Edging meets the skirt bottom. Machine sew the trim in place. With right sides together, sew from about 2" (5 cm) below the waistband down to the bottom of the skirt. Where the skirt has a raw edge below the waist band, sew both sides under (figure d).

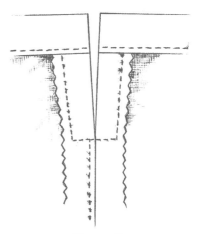

(figure d)
Sew the skirt back seam, leaving the waist opening.

14. Following the Cuff Beaded Edging instructions (page 34), bead the bottom of the skirt edging with size 11/12 seed beads. When you get to the points, add beaded fringe (page 118). Use the accent beads for this (figure e).

(figure e)
Add beaded fringe to the skirt.

15. Hand sew snaps in place on the waistband and sew a button on one side of the waistband. Place skirt on Elizabethe.

THE VEST

1. The vest is made using the Jacket Upper Bodice, Jacket Lower Front, and Jacket Back (on pages 111–112). This is from the jacket used for Helen and is simply redrawn. Follow the illustration (figure f) and draw the pattern for the vest. Use tissue paper or pattern drafting paper to redraw these pieces. Shorten the Jacket Lower Front and Jacket Back so that the vest will fall just below the doll's waist. Draw a narrow pattern for the trim for the front of the vest. In the illustration, you will see a dashed line to represent this trim. Do not make the vest pattern piece narrower at center front. The trim is fused on top of the vest fabric piece.

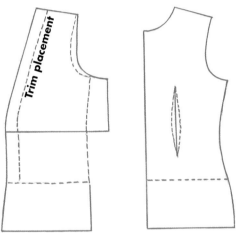

(figure f)
Draw the vest pattern using Helen's jacket pattern pieces.

2. Cut out two sets of the front and back pieces from the fabrics you have chosen. On the trim, before cutting it out, iron some double-sided iron-on stabilizer on the wrong side of the fabric. Cut out two sets of trim, peel off the paper backing, and iron in place on the fronts of the vest fabric shapes.

3. Sew the shoulder and side seams on both sets of the fabric shapes. With right sides together, pin one set to the other. Sew all the way around the outer edges of the vest, leaving the armholes open. Turn the vest right side out through one of the armholes and iron it flat.

4. Hand sew the armholes together by turning under the raw edges as you sew them.

5. Following the Cuff Beaded Edging instructions (page 34), bead along the bottom edge of the vest and up around the outer edge of the trim.

6. To embellish the vest, some of it has to be done after it is on the doll, but the beaded fringe can be made first. Thread up a beading needle with 1 yard (91 cm) of beading thread. Tie a knot in the end and anchor the thread at the back of the vest, opposite the edge where you want the fringe. Take the needle through the vest and come out at the edge. String on several size 11/12 seed beads, then a size 6/7, more size 11/12 beads, another size 6/7, and so on. At the end of the length you want, add an accent bead and then a "stop" bead. Skip the "stop" bead and go up the beads you just added and into the vest edge. Create as many of these fringes as you like until you have the look you want. Do the same on the other side of the vest.

(figure g)
Add beaded fringe to the vest hem.

7. Place the vest onto the doll. Hand sew a piece of costume jewelry on one side of the vest, near the doll's bust. On one bottom edge of the vest, hand sew another piece of costume jewelry. Under this, string on beads to create the loops that you see on the sample doll (figure g). Go from one side to the other.

Costume jewelry is so fun to use on dolls. I love going to thrift stores and buying old earrings and necklaces. I take them apart and use the bits as embellishments for my dolls. Old rings can become crowns for a smaller doll.

8. Trace the General Shape pattern (page 115) eight times onto the sleeve fabric. Fold each shape in half diagonally as shown (figure h), with right sides together, and sew with a 1/8" (3 mm) seam allowance, leaving one area open for turning. Turn each shape right side out through this opening and hand sew the openings closed.

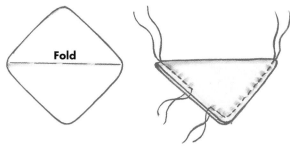

(figure h)
Fold the shapes in half diagonally and stitch.

9. Place two of the shapes together and sew a gathering stitch at the back, catching the shapes together. Pull and you will get a nice looking cluster. Create four of these clusters and hand sew all of them to the vest, at the shoulders, to represent cap sleeves.

Stefania Morgante created a collage bodice using feathers, dried clusters from trees, organza, and crocheted wire.

Another great idea is to encase fibers under organza, as Stephanie Novatski did with her Firefly Fairy.

The Shoes

1. Using the Shoe Top, Shoe Sole, Heel Side, Heel Front, Heel Back, Heel Bottom (page 112), and Boot Top (page 115) trace all of the pieces onto the wrong side of the red cotton fabric. When you get to the toe of the Shoe Top, round it out (figure i).

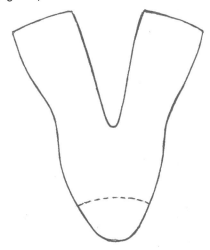

(figure i)
Draw the toe on the Shoe Top.

2. Follow the instructions for sewing the shoes found in Chapter 2 (page 36). The only difference will be that you will not have to sew the toe opening. Slip the shoes onto the doll's feet.

3. Trace four Boot Top pattern pieces (page 115) for the top of the shoes (figure i). This turns the shoes into boots, which were more common during this era. Double the fabric and sew along the entire length of seam #1 on two of the pieces. On the remaining two boot pieces, sew seam #1 but leave an opening in the center of the seam. Cut them out of the fabric using 1/8" (3 mm) seam allowances.

4. Open up each of the boot pieces and, with right sides together, pin two pieces to each other, making sure that each pair has a piece with an opening in the seam. Sew all the way around the outer edges. Turn the boots right side out through the opening you created earlier. Iron flat and pin the boots to the doll's legs, just above the heels of the shoes. Hand sew the boots in place using a ladder stitch (page 119).

5. Cut two 16" (40.6 cm) lengths of ribbon to match the doll's boots. Starting at the top, hand sew the ribbons to the edges of the boot openings, crisscrossing them as you go down the boot front. When you get to the top of the foot, tie the ribbons into bows and tack them in place.

6. Thread up a beading needle with 1 yard (91 cm) of beading thread. Place a knot in the end and tack it into the foot, under the shoe so that it does not show, at the top edge of the boot, by the ribbon. Using the size 6/7 and 11/12 seed beads, add embellishments along the edge of the shoe and the boot. Start by placing a size 6/7 bead, then a size 11/12 bead on the needle and thread. Skip the size 11/12 and go through the size 6/7 bead and then insert the needle and thread into the shoe. Move over 3/8" (1 cm) along the edge of the boot and do another bead stack. Continue this along the edge of the boot top and shoe top.

Anne van der Kley used the jacket pattern to create a patchwork vest. Note the unique way Anne created the doll's hair with threads stitched together on a serger.

Cody Goodin cut craft foam into shapes, glued them together, and came up with really fun platform sandals. Cody also gave his doll an African 'fro, which was very popular in the late '60s and early '70s.

Sally Lampi made really simple shoes by sewing loops along the lining of the sole. Then the sole was sewn to the bottom of the shoe. Ribbons were threaded through the loops, which created a sandal effect. The work is simple and just the right touch for this fun doll.

The Hair and Headpiece

1. Color the face as you wish. I copied the way Zandra Rhodes used to wear eye make-up during the late '60 s and early '70s. Eyes were very important during this time period, with heavy make-up and false eyelashes. Lips were paler, as were eyebrows. Follow the instructions in Chapter 2 (page 22) for coloring a doll face.

2. If you are using the Tibetan goat hair, follow steps 4, 5, and 6 (page 97), for cutting and attaching this type of hair to the head.

3. Cut a 20" (50.8 cm) length of yarn and a 1½" × 24" (3.8 × 61 cm) strip from the silk scarf. Tie the scarf and yarn together near each end, leaving a bit of the ends loose for embellishments. The sample doll used Macao ribbon yarn.

4. Thread up a beading needle with 1 yard (91 cm) of beading thread. Tie a knot in the long end and attach it to the knot at one end of the headband. Place 9 of the size 11/12 seed beads on the needle and thread and wrap around the headband, twisting this as you tack in place (figure j). Add nine more seed beads, changing colors if you wish, and continue around the headband wrap When you get to the end tie knot, leaving at least 3" (7.6 cm) free. Tie the headband around the doll's head and tack in place.

(figure j)
Wrap beading around the silk and yarn.

5. Add beaded fringe from the knot created when the wrap was placed on her head.

The Purse

1. Create another piece of collage fabric with a 9" × 4" (22.9 × 10.2 cm) piece of batik, snippets of fabrics, lace, ribbons, threads, and yarns, and the tulle or fine netting on top.

2. Using the General Shape pattern piece (page 115), cut two of these shapes from the collage fabric. Pin the shapes together, right sides together, and sew along three of the edges. Turn right side out and turn down the raw edge. Hand sew a hem and, at the same time, sew beads along the opening.

3. Cut two pieces of yarn, each 6" (15.2 cm) long and add seed beads as you did on her headpiece by wrapping the yarn with sets of nine seed beads. Hand sew each end of the beaded yarn to the sides of the purse, to create a handle. Add some beaded fringe if desired (figure k).

(figure k)
Embellish the handle with beads.

4. Hand sew a tassel to the bottom point of the purse. To make your own tassel wrap yarn, fabric scraps, and beaded threads around a small piece of cardboard. Slip the fibers off the cardboard and secure them at the top by wrapping it with yarn. If you have added beaded threads, do not cut the bottom of the tassel.

Congratulations, you now have a beautiful, hip doll straight from the '60s with a touch of the '70s and a bit from the twenty-first century.

GALLERY

SOWMYA

Diane Leftwich

The artist writes:

Making this doll was so much fun. I thought of all the things that reminded me of the "hippie" era and then just went with the flow—kurdas, Indian embroidery, natural fibers, paisley, ponchos, toe sandals, daisy chains, and tie-dyeing.

I gathered all the different types of silk I could find and dyed them using shibori and tie-dyeing techniques. These fabrics were then torn into strips, some were stamped with fabric paint, and pieces were then sewn together to make the pants. The same fabrics were also used for her bag and headscarf. Old Indian embroideries filled with shisha mirrors inspired Sowmya's kurda. I used naïve stitching with different textured threads on layers of colored velvet.

The motifs on her clothes and bag are free-motion embroideries, some using stamps as a base pattern. Motifs on the kurda have had the fabric cut away from behind, allowing you to see through to colors beneath. The poncho was constructed by weaving yarns together with a very finely teased out silk cap overlay. This was sandwiched between water-soluble film and machine stitched to resemble large needle knitting. The daisies were sewn onto georgette and water-soluble film, then cut out and attached to stems made from fabric and thread cords.

Sowmya's sandals are several layers of soft leather glued together. This allowed the straps to be neatly secured between the layers, and decorated with Indian decals. Her hair was made from wefted mohair with a wonderful shibori dyed headscarf tied around her head. Bells and bangles completed the "hippie" feel.

FLOWER

Elise Peeples

The artist writes:

I treated this entire project as a "hippie collage." I reduced the doll pattern to 75 percent. I used lightweight denim from an old tote bag for the blue jeans. To create the appliqué for the blue jeans, I drew a collage picture and colored it with iridescent watercolors. I reduced the image size using an ink-jet printer, then printed it onto fusible fabric. I cut the image apart, fused it to the right leg, and embellished it with machine embroidery and beads. The motifs on the left leg were cut from several printed fabrics, applied to the jeans, embroidered and beaded. I added embroidered trim as fringe around the hems and used tiny brass brads for the button fly. The blouse was made from a discarded gauze top and antique sari border trim. I hand embroidered fifteen shisha mirrors, which were cut from a lightweight metal sheet using a paper punch. The belt is another embroidered trim backed with synthetic suede. The vest is lightweight leather with hand-dyed lace trim. The earrings, bracelet, and peace sign are cut from printed tin. The tote is made from a hand-woven fabric. Inside is a tiny edition of the *Tao Te Ching*, a vial of patchouli, a ball of sea grass, a feather, a pebble from the Washington coast, and a tiny silk bag of crystals.

CHELSEA

Nancy Palomino

The artist writes:

For extra money while going to college in the late
'60s, I made hippie clothing, earrings, and macramé
belts. Making this doll brought back memories of that
colorful time in my life. After the doll body was sewn
and stuffed, I made the clothing patterns by draping,
cutting, and basting muslin to fit properly.

Variegated silk velvet and burnout velvet are used for
the pants. They are embellished with hand-dyed venice
lace and small bells. The cotton T-shirt fabric and all
lace embellishments were dyed in one session. A lace
heart is hand sewn to the front of the shirt.

For the tunic, I chose the ultimate collage: crazy
patch. I love to maintain a stash of buttons, beads,
charms, threads, lace, and ribbons for this type of
project. Patches of silk, velvet, rayon, and hand-
dyed cottons are sewn onto a base fabric that is a
bit larger than the pattern pieces. Many hours were
spent on appliqué, beading shisha, needle lace,
and silk-ribbon embroidery. Machine and hand
embroidery was stitched with variegated cotton and
rayon threads. Some of the fabric was embellished
with bonding powder and metal leaf or stamped
with luminescent paint. The tunic pattern pieces were
cut from this embellished fabric, stitched together,
and lined.

Her hat is made of silk velvet with a ribbon trim and
silk ribbon flowers. Free-motion stitched leaves and
beads complete the embellishments.

The Birkenstock-style shoes are made with cork and
foam soles and buckled, thin leather straps.

Her finished head was sewn on last. Red mohair was
attached and braided. Charms were sewn on as earrings. A macramé strap completes the bead and
charm embellished purse.

WILLOW

Dale Rollerson

The artist writes:

This doll was a tremendous challenge for me as I am not an experienced doll maker but a textile artist. My friend, Jaslyn Pearce, actually made the doll for me to make sure I got started.

I recently purchased an embellisher and used it to make her knickers. I embellished merino wool onto Romeo water-soluble fabric and then reapplied it to scrim (butter muslin) with a few extra trimmings and some hand stitching. They are all hidden—but the added layers will keep her warm!

The bodice was similar to an art to wear piece I was creating at the same time. I machine stitched lots of threads, Angelina, and silk fibers between sheets of Romeo, then soaked it in cold water to remove the film. It was molded to her body and let dry so it would retain that shape.

I knitted some fishnet leg warmers and made a petal overlay with different weights of hand-dyed silk. A machine-stitched cord is wrapped around her waist. I knitted short ends of silk thread for her coat. Her hat is free-motion machine stitched, hand-dyed velvet. Her bag and shoes are both made on the embellisher with some lace stitched on thermogauze that is felted into the surface.

DESTINY'S CHILD

Diane Evdokimoff

The artist writes:

This theme gave me the opportunity to play with several processes from fabric dying to free-motion machine embroidery and beading. I chose a simple method of dressing her using flared jeans, a T-shirt, and a vest.

Her top is fine T-shirt fabric. I wet it, twisted it into a spiral, and applied dyes, with the color running out from the center like spokes on a wheel. When the fabric was opened, it created a spiral design, reminiscent of the psychedelic prints of the era. Once it was sewn, I simply cut into the hem of the T-shirt to create the fringe.

The jeans are embellished with tiny daisies and some free-motion machine embroidery. A few hearts were ironed on using a double-sided bonding sheet. Her vest is made with leather scraps and embellished with beading and rick-rack. The purse was made from a scrap of felt and marbleized fabric. Beaded fringe finished the bottom edge of the purse.

The sandals were made using a piece of leather that was cut and glued in two layers. The straps were then sewn in place. Her toenails are painted to match her fingernails.

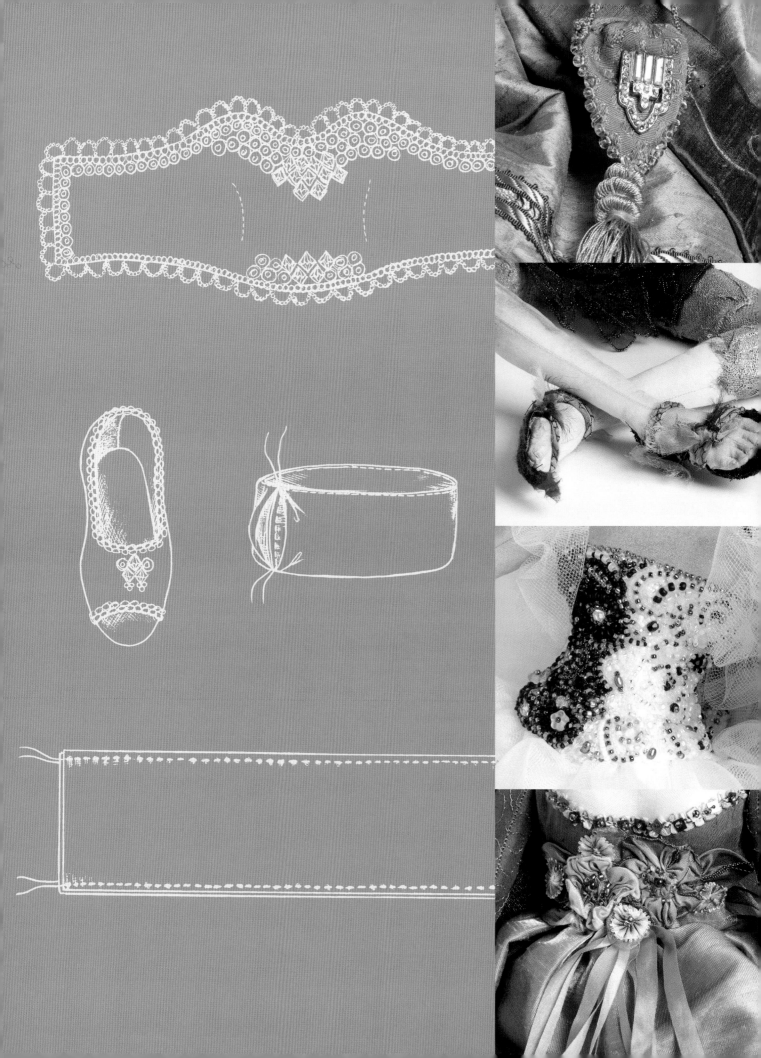

CHAPTER 4

DRAPING FOR A FORMAL AFFAIR: WORKING WITH BEADS, LACE, SATIN, AND SILK

When it comes to draping, dolls are a whole lot easier to deal with than humans. In the real world of fashion, draping temperamental models can be a real pain. It is a highly specialized skill that is extremely difficult to master; plus artists need to learn to negotiate with some of the fragile egos that walk the runway. In the doll world, many of us who design our own creations use draping more than any other technique for making garments. And our dolls are happy with anything we do.

Draping is sculpting with fabric. Soft fabrics work best, and for our purpose, they will make it easier to learn this technique.

CHRISTINA LEFEVRE

Elegant, sophisticated, regal. These words seem to describe the doll for this chapter. Working with silks and beads gives a feeling of satisfaction when the project is finished.

MATERIALS

basic body with straight legs (pages 12–23)

stand for 18" (45.7 cm) doll

½ yard (46 cm) copper-colored silk dupioni

¼ yard (23 cm) bridal lace

¼ yard (23 cm) silk satin or silk charmeuse, natural colored or color to match your theme

sewing machine thread in color to match the silk dupioni

upholstery or strong quilting thread in color to match silk dupioni

size 11/12 seed beads in two colors

size 8/9 seed beads in two colors

size 14/15 seed beads in two colors

accent beads: drops, flower-shaped, 6 mm (¼") marguerites

4 mm (5/32") bicone crystals in two colors

pieces of costume jewelry or decorative buttons for dress, hat, and shrug

paper toweling

mohair for hair

thread to match mohair

TOOLS

basic clothing and sewing kits (pages 10–11)

THE PATTERN DRAPING

1. Make the doll body using the straight leg pattern. Assemble the body, but wait to attach the arms after the gown is made and placed on the body. Secure the doll body with a stand so it is easy to work with. Decide what type of evening dress you want and collect the fabrics, paper toweling, mechanical pencil, and straight pins. You will be creating your own evening gown using the draping method.

2. Cut a piece of paper toweling the size you want for the costume you have in mind. Arrange the paper toweling around the body. Pin it in place (figure a), cutting it to fit at the back. The sample doll will have a separate bodice, so a shorter length of paper toweling is pinned around her bodice. Pin a longer piece of paper toweling to the body for the skirt, depending on the type of gown you are creating. Cut it to the length you want.

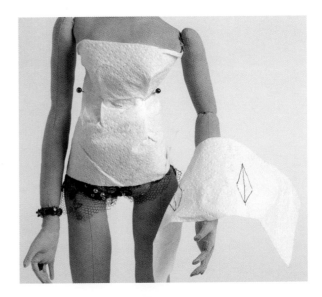

(figure a)
Pin the paper toweling to the doll.

3. Mark the seams and darts on the pinned paper toweling with a mechanical pencil. Pin in the darts (figure b). As you pin the darts, make any corrections needed. Remove the paper toweling from the body and cut out the shapes from the paper toweling. These are your paper patterns.

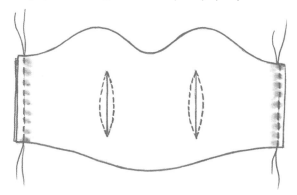

(figure b)
Pin the darts and mark the seams on the front and back.

If you are going to bead the bodice, make the pattern about ¼" (6 mm) larger. The beadwork pulls the fabric in a bit. Without the extra width, the bodice would be too small when placed on the doll.

THE BODICE

1. Pin the paper toweling pattern to the silk dupioni fabric and cut out the pieces.

2. Sew in the darts and sew the seams together. Place the bodice on the body again to make sure it all fits. A beaded bodice needs to be lined to give the bodice more stability to handle the weight of the beads. Cut out and assemble a second bodice. Sew the two bodice pieces together, right sides together. Turned the joined bodice right side out.

3. Thread up a beading needle with 1 yard (91 cm) of beading thread. Place a knot in one end and tack it to the underside of the bodice. Stitching through both layers of the bodice fabric, bead the upper edge of the bodice. Following the bead embroidery instructions (page 34), bead the bodice. The sample doll has three rows of backstitched beading along the top edge, one row of picots above the top row of backstitching, stacked single stitchbeading, and a simple fringe (figure c).

(figure c)
Graph of beading techniques on the bodice.

A close-up of the beaded bodice shows how beading can bring elegance to a simple garment.

The Skirt

1. The skirt is slightly gathered at the waist. With the elaborate bodice, the skirt will not be the focal point. A full skirt would overpower the gown.

2. Cut the paper-toweling skirt pattern from the silk dupioni. Machine gather it at the waist.

3. If desired, dye the bridal lace to match or contrast the skirt fabric. Machine-hem the bottom of the skirt, using a matching color thread. Lace will cover the stitching, so there is no need to hand sew a hem. Along the bottom of the skirt, hand sew the bridal lace in place. With right sides together, machine sew the center back seam from the hem to the waist. Turn, right side out, and place the skirt on the body. Pull the gathering threads to fit at the waist. Hand sew the skirt directly to the body.

Some of the dyed bridal lace was used for Christina's underwear. The lace was hand sewn onto the doll. It is very easy to do and adds a lovely touch. Adding underwear is explained in Chapter 5 (pages 88–89).

4. Place the bodice onto the doll and hand sew it together at the back with the beaded edges overlapping at the back and over the skirt.

The Bracelets

1. It is much easier to sew the bracelets to the wrists before attaching the arms. Anchor the beading thread at the wrist and thread up enough beads on a beading needle to wrap around the wrist.

2. Insert the needle through the first beads added, to make a circle and tack this row to her arm in at least three places. Thread up another row of beads and attach them to the arm. Add a third row. Anchor that row to the arm.

For this doll made by Dorice Larkin, the entire bodice is embroidered with beads.

3. Embellish the bracelet with marguerites. Come out a bead from her wrist and into a marguerite. Add an anchor bead (size 14/15 seed bead). Skip the seed bead and push the needle back through the marguerite and into the bead on her wrist. Insert the needle through five seed beads on the wrist and add another marguerite. Continue around the wrist, adding more marguerites.

A marguerite is a copy of a vintage bead made by Swarovski. The company has started making them again, and they are beautiful accents for any project. They are shaped like flowers and come in several sizes.

THE SHRUG

Rather than sleeves for this doll, a shrug added a nice finishing touch.

1. Cut 17" (43.2 cm) long by 6" (15.2 cm) wide piece from both the silk dupioni and the silk satin (for the lining). With right sides together, sew along the two long edges, leaving open at each short end (figure d).

(figure d)
Join the shrug to the lining along the long edges.

2. Turn the shrug right side out through one end, and with right sides of the silk dupioni together, sew across the ends. This closes the piece into a tube shape (figure e). Hand sew the lining closed.

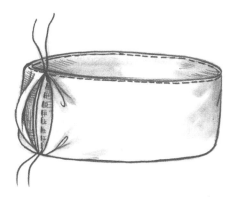

(figure e)
Join the short ends of the silk dupioni.

3. Place the shrug on the doll and pin the two pieces together at the back. Hand sew these two sections together with strong thread. When you slip this off the doll, it will look like a bow.

4. To hide the stitches, hand sew a decorative button or piece of costume jewelry at the center and then create some beaded fringe (step 6, page 54) to hang down from the centerpiece.

If the beads on the bridal lace and the costume jewelry do not match the colors on the dress, color them with markers. As long as the garments are not laundered, the color will last the lifetime of the doll. You do not need special markers. Any colored marker will work. The pearls on the bridal lace and the costume jewelry of Christina's shrug and headpiece were colored with Pantone markers.

Another idea for a finishing garment is adding a cape. Desiree Simpson created a lovely cape for her doll. Note the beautiful silk ribbon work on the bodice of the gown.

A fun example of draping a figure is Ann Maulin's doll. Ann draped the doll with fabrics, rather than paper toweling. She used a combination of organza, scrim, and silk.

The Shoes

1. Follow the instructions for the shoes in Chapter 2 (page 36), but omit the heels. If you are making the shoes from the silk dupioni, you will want to stick with flats, rather than heels. Christina is a dancing girl, so flats are definitely what she wants to wear.

2. After the shoe is made, collect your beading materials and tools. Using the beading needle and thread, anchor the thread with several small stitches at the back of the shoe (where the heel would be). Thread up about thirteen size 11/12 seed beads and backstitch them around the top edge of the. Do two rows of beading. You can change bead colors with each row, if you wish.

3. Starting at the heel, come out of a bead on the top row and add five size15 seed beads. Skip a bead that is attached to the shoe and go into the next attached bead with the needle and thread. Come out that same bead. Add five more size 14/15 seed beads and make another picot. Continue all the way around the shoe top adding the five-bead picots.

4. At the center front of the shoe top, add some crystals and single-bead stacks (figure f).

(figure f)
Add crystals and single bead stacks to the shoes.

5. At the toe, add beaded edging (page 34).

It is easier to bead the shoes before placing them on the foot. Once beaded, slip the shoes onto the feet, and then tack them in place with a needle and thread.

The Hat and Hair

1. Collect the silk dupioni. Cut a piece 17" (43.2 cm) long by 4" (10.2 cm) wide. Fold it in half with the short ends meeting. Sew from the opening to the folded end. Repeat on the other side (figure g).

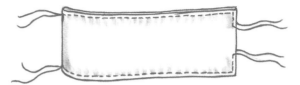

(figure g)
Sew the long edges of the silk dupioni fabric strip.

2. Turn the fabric piece right side out and close up the opening by hand sewing with a needle and thread. Twist the piece into the shape you want and secure the shape's folds by hand sewing with a needle and thread. Before attaching the hat to the doll's head, the hair needs to be sewn onto the head.

3. Following the directions in Chapter 2 (page 39), attach the hair. Arrange in the style you want, then secure with a needle and thread.

4. Once the hair is where you want it, hand sew the hat to the head. As you sew the hat in place, secure the doll's hair into its style. Hand sew a decorative button, or costume jewelry, to the hat.

For Christina's decorative jewelry pieces, the starting point was an inexpensive bracelet strung on stretchy plastic. The plastic was cut away, leaving the beautiful pieces for accents on the purse, hat, shrug, and skirt. These bracelets are great sources of fun accents for dolls.

Michele Naylor has used a piece of crinkled silk to make a unique hat for her doll.

THE PURSE

1. The squarish General Shape pattern piece (page 115) comes into play again. This time it is used as is. Cut out two shapes from the silk dupioni and two from the silk satin. With right sides together, sew the dupioni shapes together, leaving one corner open (figure h). Repeat with the silk satin shapes.

(figure h)
Join the silk dupioni shapes and the silk satin shapes together.

2. Turn the silk satin piece right side out and slip it into the silk dupioni piece, right sides together. Pin it in place. Sew along the raw edges, leaving open at one corner (figure i).

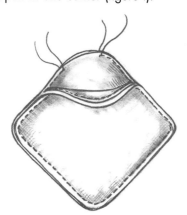

(figure i)
Sew the silk satin into the silk duponi.

3. Turn the purse right side out. Push out the seam with a pair of hemostats and hand sew the opening closed. With a warm iron, press the top of the purse down. The lining will show, which gives a nice contrast.

4. Use the size 11/12 seed beads and drop beads to sew a bead edging along the edges of the turned down part of the purse. Follow the Cuff Beaded Edging instructions (page 34), but change the look by adding a drop bead where the second ("up") bead would be. On the front of the purse, add three marguerite beads or a decorative button.

5. The handle for the purse is very simple. Using a beading needle, attach beading thread at one side of the purse. String on three size 11/12 seed beads, three drop beads, five size 11/12 seed beads, three drop beads, three size 11/12 seed beads, three drop beads, five size 11/12 seed beads, and three drop beads. Then add three size 6/7 seed beads, three accent beads, three size 6/7 seed beads. End with three drop beads and three size 11/12 seed beads. Attach the strand to the other side of the purse. Christina's purse has a double strap. Create the same pattern as before and attach it to the other side of the purse.

Barbara Willis used a beautiful piece of antique costume jewelry as the accent on her doll's purse.

GALLERY

qSABELLA

Ray Slater

The artist writes:

Isabella's inspiration came from the paintings of William Larkin, famous for his full-length portraits of sixteenth-century Elizabethan nobility. I wanted to capture the essence of the costumes worn in the reign of Elizabeth I but with a contemporary twist by using modern embroidery techniques. The body, arms, and legs are metallic silk organza backed with muslin and free-motion machine embroidered into a pattern with metallic thread.

The underskirt is made by stitching textured threads onto silk metallic organza and is trimmed with a deep gold lace edging. Using Elizabethan textile motifs as a reference, the overskirt and bodice front are created by layering two pieces of nylon organza together, free-motion embroidering a motif in metallic thread, and melting away the background with a soldering iron. Strips of knotted nylon organza are used for the hair and more cutwork motifs make a headdress.

The Masked Dancer

Leta Benedict

The artist writes:

This was an interesting doll for me to work on. Many of my original plans needed to be reworked. The only original concept that survived was to work in whites and creams. Her mask and boots were sculpted in paper clay and then painted white using Neopaque. On the mask, I added gold by stamping, then used a brush to add color around the eyes and nose using a Pearl Ex metallic gold stamp pad. The small bells were also painted white to soften the look. The boots were finished with gathers of organdy ribbon and beads. With those two pieces done, the fun began with costuming.

Her sleeves are made of dyed bias-cut silk ribbon and an antique handkerchief that was cut in two. Her bodice and waist were adorned with gathers of organdy ribbon. The skirts are layers of beaded lace and toile that are cut into long individual points, along with feathers and ivory beads. She has a purse hanging from her left arm that was made from scraps of the lace used for the first layer of her skirt. Beads were added to dress it up. The only thing left to do is to make her a dance partner to take her outstretched hand.

DOROTHEA GRACE

Deb Jensen

The artist writes:

Dorothea Grace pays homage to my grandmother Grace who always looked like she stepped right out of a bandbox. Whenever I visited her, she let me tag along to her hairdresser, play with her jewelry, and experiment with cosmetics at her very "Hollywood" three-paneled, lighted, and mirrored dressing table. I pictured Dorothea Grace attending a gala opening and began the creative process.

Her panties are made from a 3" (7.5 cm) -wide piece of gathered lace and painted with sunset gold Lumiere. One of my grandmother's pink formal gowns with layers of tulle inspired the gown. I adore Jacquard's halo pink gold Lumiere and used it to paint the silk chiffon skirt, beaded Venice lace bodice and straps, and iridescent tulle overskirt. Highlights are added with halo violet gold, pearlescent magenta, and metallic gold Lumieres along with a bit of rich medium aztec gold Textile Color.

For the skirt, I used paper toweling to make a pattern draft and then made a muslin sample so I could do any needed adjustments. Darts were essential to keep the line smooth and sleek and not hide her tiny (and much-envied by me) waist. I added a knee-length slit in back. I also stitched darts into the bodice for a snug fit. As Dorothea couldn't afford a pair of Jimmy Choo shoes, I hand-beaded shoes using seed, bugle, Miracle, and accent beads on pink ultrasuede. The soles and heels are made from combining violet, fuschia, and rose Premo Sculpey.

I hand-stamped a design into each heel. The purse uses the same techniques as the shoes but features a pink satin lining. Hand-beaded bracelets and necklace and earrings from my stash of 1960s costume jewelry complete her outfit.

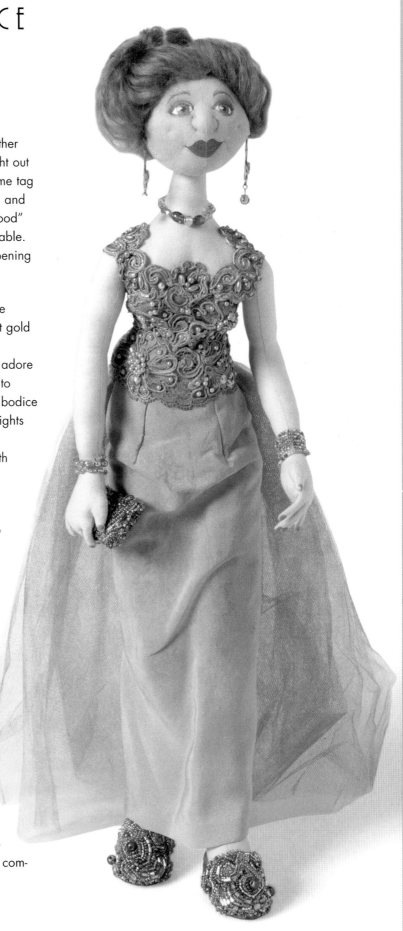

ADRIENNE AT THE QUEEN'S GARDEN PARTY

Carol Petefish Ayotte

The artist writes:

Adrienne's body is made from 100 percent white Kona cotton, and painted using a diluted solution of sienna, ochre, and white Jacquard Dye-Na-Flow paints. Her face was tinted with oil pastel pencils, Prisma pencils, and Tsukineko fabric markers.

The pantaloons and shoes are made from a frosted cotton fabric painted with aqua and purple dye. They were stamped using Jacquard pads, and drizzled with Jacquard pearl Lumiere paints.

The slip is purple hand-painted taffeta. The net crinoline is a piece of presparkled fabric made into a double layer to add fullness to the outer skirt. I fashioned her outer skirt from a scarf, hand-painted using Jacquard paints and dyes from Things Japanese. The bodice and the hat's body are both made from hand-painted silk; I applied salt to some areas to create a dotted effect. Beads and sequins are added as embellishments.

Adrienne's hat is made using a straw hat crown for shape. I added fusible pellon to shape the brim. The roses on her hat are white organza ribbon dyed to match her dress. Her gloves are made of wedding silk, while her evening bag is made of beads using a right-angle weaving technique to make a smooth surface effect. Her purple necklace and bracelets—an heirloom lent to her by her Aunt Harriet for her special day at Buckingham Palace—are made of seed beads.

A Formal Affair on Planet Zenairia

Judi Korona

The artist writes:

When I design a costume, I usually start with a sketch and work from there. I don't get overly concerned about my designs taking a different path as I create. If you trust in your instincts and let it happen, you will always be delighted with the results.

Using paper towels, I draped the figure and made a "sloper." Paper towels are an inexpensive way of designing clothing. I find it beneficial to label each piece as I make it. These are saved and can be used in other projects.

Silk is a favorite fabric and it lends itself to tiny work. The center panel of her dress was dyed using a marbling technique. A mixture of sodium alginate was made, then dollops of Jacquard's Dye-Na-Flow were added to the surface. The colors were swirled around a bit using a skewer. The silk fabric was then laid gently on the surface of the dye mixture, tapped down a little, then lifted gently up, and laid flat to dry. Once dry, it's rinsed in warm water and the sodium alginate is washed away.

CHAPTER 5

FAIRY GATHERING: STYLING A WHIMSICAL ENSEMBLE

Let us leave the world of traffic jams, noise, smog, and mortgage payments. Come to a land of all things magical, a place with breathtaking forests, unicorns, centaurs, elves, and, most exquisitely, fairies. As a child, these were my favorite playmates.

In this chapter, you will learn to create ethereal effects with dyeing, painting, and stamping. Let us dream of wings and wonder as an enchanting creature takes flight.

GOLENDRIAL

Some grownups wag their fingers (don't you hate that?) and say "fairies do not exist." Others will give you the Look and say that fairies are imaginary friends. Do not believe them. Would you be able to see Golendrial if they were telling the truth? My mother and grandmother never denied that fairies exist. In fact, my Grandmother Lefever regaled me with wonderful stories about fairies that lived nearby.

MATERIALS

doll body with straight or jointed legs (pages 12–23)

4" × 6" (10.2 × 15.2 cm) extra doll body fabric for ears

¼ yard (23 cm) of white 100% cotton for corset and shoe tops

¼ yard (23 cm) of white or natural colored silk crepe de Chine for skirt

⅓ yard (30.5 cm) cream-colored organza for overskirt and wings

12" (30.5 cm) square of lace fabric for bodice and sleeves

6" (15.2 cm) piece of 3" (7.6 cm) -wide lace for underwear

4" (10.2 cm) square of stretch velvet for purse

scraps of colored silk fabrics for berries, flowers

cloth for wiping ash off skirt fabric

stuffing such as Fairfield Polyfil

machine-sewing threads to match fabrics

upholstery thread to match hair

variegated sewing machine threads for flowers, such as Superior Threads Rainbows #816

metallic sewing machine thread for flowers, such as Superior Threads Metallic #11

Kreinik medium #16 braid in Heather

YLI Candlelight Metallic Yarns in gold, green, and pink

size 14/15 seed beads in five colors for flowers (size 11/12 if you are more comfortable with larger beads)

size 14/15 green seed beads for leaves (size 11/12 if you are more comfortable with larger beads)

size 11/12 crystal-colored size seed beads

size 11/12 gold charlottes

4 mm crystals in various colors for flower centers

small drop beads for baubles

1 accent bead and 1 larger drop bead for purse

beading thread

24-gauge floral wire in color to match your theme, for wings (*Note: Beading wire comes on a spool and is used mainly for beads.*)

double-sided, water-soluble stabilizer such as Floriani Wet N Gone Fusible Dissolvable Stabilizer, Freudenberg Solusheet/Vilene 541, Mokuba Free Lace, or Brother Foundation Aqua-Melt Water-Soluble Stabilizer

1 pipe cleaner for ears

4" (10.2 cm) square of Tibetan goat hair

paper toweling

several small bells

Jacquard Lumiere paint: halo pink gold, halo violet gold, metallic gold, pearlescent magenta, pearlescent violet, sunset gold, super copper

Jacquard Dye-Na-Flow paint: cranberry red, golden yellow, violet

Jacquard Pearl-EX: antique bronze, brilliant gold, super bronze, super russet

TOOLS

basic clothing, fabric-dyeing, and sewing kits (pages 10–11)

free-motion or darning presser foot

embroidery foot (optional)

lucet (optional)

candle and tin pie plate

You have the option of wiring the fairy body or using the jointed legs so that your doll can sit.

THE EARS

1. After the doll is made, trace two Ear patterns (page 107) onto the wrong side of the flesh-colored fabric that you used for the body. Double the fabric, right sides together, and machine sew around the ears, leaving open where marked. Cut out, using a scant 1/8" (3 mm) seam allowance, and turn the ear right side out through the opening.

2. Using a mechanical pencil, draw the outline of the ear lobe (stitching lines on the pattern piece) on the inner side of each ear. With the sewing machine, topstitch along this line. As you do this, leave room between the stitching line and the edge of the ear along the inner edge, for the pipe cleaner to be inserted. Measure the ear with the pipe cleaner and cut to fit the ear (figure a), allowing a bit of extra length at each end (1/4" or 6 mm, total), to be turned back.

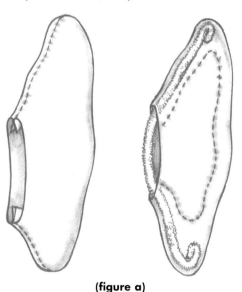

(figure a)
Measure the pipe cleaner.

3. Pinch under the tip at each end of a pipe cleaner and insert it into the ear. The pipe cleaner fits just along the inside edge of the ear. With a needle and thread, close up the opening of the ear using a ladder stitch (page 119).

4. Attach the ears to the side of the head and bend them as shown (figure b). Although the photo shows the hair attached, leave that step for the end of the doll-making process.

(figure b)
Attach and shape the ears as desired.

THE UNDERWEAR

1. Pin the 6" (15.2 cm) piece of lace to the doll. Hand sew (tack) it in place with a needle and thread (figure c).

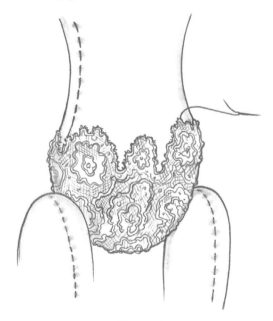

(figure c)
Sew the lace underwear to the body.

2. Wrap the 12" (30.5 cm) square of lace around the entire body at the bust, overlapping at the back, and cut it to fit. The lace ends at the waist. Wrap the leftover pieces around the arms and cut them to fit (figure d). Pin the pieces in place and hand sew the back closed on the bodice. Hand sew the sleeves to the arms. Tuck under the raw edges as you hand sew them in place.

(figure d)
Cover the bodice with lace.

THE SKIRT AND BODICE FABRIC PREPARATION

1. If you want to dye the skirt fabric, use the golden yellow Dye-Na-Flow paint as follows: Wet the silk crepe de Chine with plain tap water. Pour the dye into a plastic container and place the silk in the dye. Squeeze out the excess dye and hang the silk to dry. To heat set the dye, simply iron it at the silk setting.

2. Tear the silk into a piece 24" × 9" (61 × 22.9 cm). Light a candle and place it in a pie tin that is filled with just a bit of water in the bottom.

3. Seal the raw edges of the silk with a candle by running each edge close to the flame. Do not let the fabric touch the flame. If the silk catches fire, immediately dip it in the water. Clean up the ash along the edge of the silk with a damp cloth.

4. Using a paintbrush and Lumiere super copper and sunset gold, paint the edge of the skirt fabric that was sealed with the candle flame. Paint a small section with the copper then the next section with the gold. Change colors as you paint along the edge of the skirt. This paint prevents further fraying and adds a nice finish to the skirt.

5. While the edge of the skirt is drying (and since you have the paints on hand) collect the white cotton fabric and lay it on a piece of plastic. Paint the cotton with sunset gold, super copper, and metallic gold.

> **TIP**
>
> *I like using my fingers to move the paint around to give a blended look.*

6. While the paint is still damp, rub in some of the Pearl-EX colors (figure e). This gives the cotton a leather look. Again, use your fingers to rub in the Pearl-EX. A darker shade of Pearl-EX will add shadows and a lighter color will add highlights. Set the cotton aside to dry.

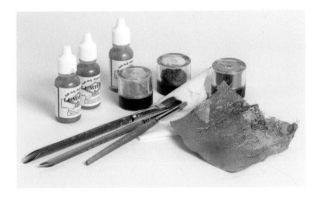

(figure e)
Transform white cotton into a leatherlike garment fabric with paints and brushes.

7. Cut a piece of the cream-colored organza 24" × 7" (61 × 17.8 cm). Cut slits along one of the long edges. These slits are random and in varying lengths.

8. Using the candle, run the edge of the organza close to the flame. The edge will melt. Be careful, organza is polyester and will be very hot until it cools. When the raw fabric edges have been sealed, hold the fabric above the flame so that the organza crinkles (figure f). If you hold it too close to the flame, it will burn a hole in it, so watch carefully as you do this.

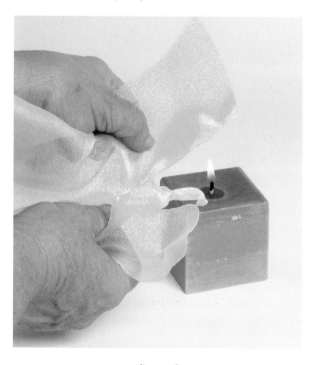

(figure f)
Singe the fabric to seal the raw edges.

THE FLOWERS AND LEAVES

1. Before the corset is made, it is best to prepare the flowers that are made using bits of fabric and free-motion embroidery work. Using a ball-point pen, trace seven flower patterns (page 115) directly onto the stabilizer. Also trace nine leaf patterns (page 115).

2. Cut out seven flowers from scraps of cotton, silk, and other fabric scraps. Place these onto another piece of water-soluble stabilizer. Place another piece of stabilizer over these flowers and pin the layers together.

3. Place variegated thread in the upper threader and metallic thread in the bobbin of your sewing machine. Lower the feed dogs and place a free-motion or darning presser foot on your machine. Set the stitch length to 0 (extremely short) and loosen the upper tension slightly.

4. To start free-motion embroidery, hang onto the ends of the bobbin and needle threads and machine sew a couple of stitches. Cut the loose thread ends, then start sewing. Outline the flower and leaf shapes first, then sew in a grid inside each shape (figure g). The other stitches can lock on to this grid. Make sure this grid touches the outline that was sewn first. If this does not happen, when the stabilizer is washed away the stitches will fall apart. Cut the threads between each shape, doing so either during the stitching or after the stabilizer is dissolved.

TIP

In free-motion machine embroidery, you control the length of the stitches when you move around the fabric. The feed dogs, which usually do this job, are lowered. If your sewing machine does not allow the feed dogs to lower, you can still do free-motion work. The important part is that the presser foot does not touch the plate of your machine. This is what allows you to control the stitches and the movement of the fabric. Move your hands slowly. If you move the fabric too quickly, the sewing machine needle will break.

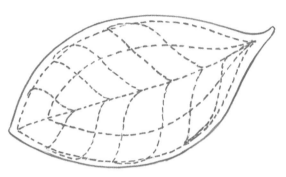

(figure g)
Stitch a flower and leaf shape, then sew a grid inside each.

5. Fill in the flowers and leaves with stitches, making sure that the lines of fill stitching overlap each other inside a shape, and also stitch through the outline of that shape.

6. When you have sewn seven free-motion flowers and nine leaves, it is time to work on the fabric flowers. Sew around the seven fabric flowers that were previously cut from the scraps of fabric and are now sandwiched inside sheets of stabilizer. Sew a few lines from the outer edge to the center of each flower. This stitching simply stabilizes the fabric and prevents fraying, plus it adds a nice touch.

7. Dissolve the stabilizer in lukewarm water. Take the flowers and leaves out of the water and rinse them under running water. Lay them on paper toweling to dry.

THE BAUBLES

1. Trace the Bauble pattern piece (page 117) onto a piece of tissue paper or pattern paper. Cut out at least eleven bauble shapes from cotton, rayon, silk, and velvet fabric scraps.

> **TIP**
>
> *If you stack three to four pieces of fabric and cut out the circles at the same time, this step will go quickly. It helps to cut out the silk and velvet pieces with pinking shears. This prevents the edges of the pieces from fraying as you sew.*

2. Thread up a beading needle with 1 yard (91 cm) of beading thread. Sew a gathering stitch around the edge of a bauble shape. Pull the threads just tight enough to allow you to place a small amount of stuffing inside. Place the stuffing in the circle and pull the threads to close the bauble opening.

3. Tuck the raw fabric edge of the bauble inside.

4. Cut a piece of YLI or Kreinik thread 12" (30.5 cm) long. Tuck one end inside the bauble. Sew the end of the length to the bauble with a needle and thread. Take a few stitches along the top of the bauble to keep the circle closed (figure h).

(figure h)
Fill the fabric circle, add the thread length, and stitch it closed.

5. Place nine seed beads of one color on the needle and thread. Move down the bauble and push the needle inside the bauble, pulling it out back at the top of the bauble. Do this several more times, randomly spaced, around the bauble.

6. Push the needle and thread inside the bauble and come out at the center of the bottom. Place a seed bead, a drop bead, and then another seed bead onto the needle and thread. Insert the needle back inside the bauble, close to where you came out, and pull the needle and thread back out at the top of the bauble.

7. Place five green seed beads on the needle and thread. Skipping the last bead, insert the needle in and out of the fourth (second to last) bead. Add three green seed beads to the needle and thread. Insert the needle and thread back into the bauble and out at the top. This creates a leaf (figure i). Make three more leaves along the top of the bauble.

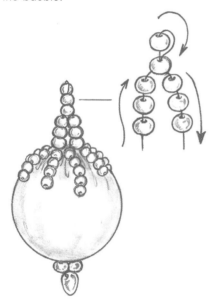

(figure i)
Define the leaves with bead strands.

8. Make another bauble and place it at the other end of the 12" (30.5 cm) piece of ribbon, thread, or yarn. Cut five more pieces of thread and add the baubles to each end of all of them. These will be placed on the corset later.

THE CORSET

1. Trace the Corset pattern pieces (pages 116–117) onto a piece of tissue paper, pattern paper, or template plastic. Cut them out. You will use these as templates.

> Cut out the darts on the template. This makes it easier to trace the darts onto the fabric.

2. Lay the Corset Front template on the wrong side of the painted cotton and trace one using a mechanical pencil. Trace one Corset Back, then flip it over and trace another Corset Back with the template wrong side up. This gives you a left and right side to the back of the corset. Be sure to trace the darts. Leave enough room to cut out the shoe pattern pieces from this fabric.

3. The embellishing is done before cutting the bodice shapes from the fabric. Place variegated thread in the upper threader of your sewing machine. Use a basic sewing thread in the bobbin. The back side of the fabric will not show.

4. Start to randomly sew up and down the fabric, on the right side. Every once in a while, add scraps of fabric and stitch over these. Along the top edge, where you think the top of the corset would be, start attaching the flowers you already made (photo of Golendrial, page 86). Save five flowers to add after the corset is sewn together.

5. Following the traced pattern on the back of the fabric, cut out the corset pieces from the embellished fabric. Machine sew all of the darts. Pin the two back pieces to the front, right sides together, and machine sew seam #3 using a 1/8" (3 mm) -wide seam allowance. Finger-press the seams flat.

6. Cut a piece of water-soluble stabilizer 4" (10.2 cm) wide by the length of the corset. Pin it in place underneath the top edge of the corset.

7. Free-motion embroider along the raw edge of the top of the corset, along both the front and backs. When you get to the front of the corset, add some of the flowers and sew them in place with free-motion stitching (figure j).

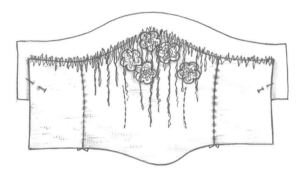

(figure j)
Free-motion embroider to finish the upper raw edge and secure the last five flowers.

8. Cut another piece of water-soluble stabilizer 4" (10.2 cm) wide by the length of the corset and pin it to the bottom of the corset. Free-motion embroider an edging along the lower edge of the corset as you did along the top. This time, add the baubles (page 91) every $3/4$"–1" (1.9–2.5 cm).

9. As you did with the baubles, machine sew leaves at each end of a 12" (30.5 cm) length of YLI or Kreinik thread or ribbon. Attach the embellished lengths to the corset, between the baubles.

10. When you get to the back opening, free-motion embroider up one side (raw edge) only. The embellished side will cover the raw edge side when it is placed on the doll.

11. Hand sew a couple of the beaded flowers (at right) on the front of the corset. Set aside the corset.

THE BEADED FLOWERS

Beaded flowers are very easy and add a nice touch to Golendrial's bracelet, corset, and neckline. Embellishments like beaded flowers can be used to hide mistakes and seams.

1. Collect the beading needle, crystals, seed beads, and thread. Cut an 18" (45.7 cm) length of beading thread and place it on the needle.

TIP

It helps to use a piece of beeswax when working with beads. The wax prevents the thread from splitting and knotting. Once the thread is on the needle, hold the start of the thread on the piece of wax with your thumb. Using your other hand, pull the thread so that it moves across the wax. Run your fingers along the thread to clean off any excess wax.

2. Place ten seed beads onto the needle and take them down, toward the tail of the thread. Tie the thread ends together with an overhand knot. This creates a circle of beads.

3. Place seven seed beads onto the needle and, skipping one bead, draw the needle through the next (second) bead. You have now made the first seven-bead picot.

4. Repeat step 3 until you have completed five picots.

5. Place the needle and thread inside the circle and add a crystal. Pull the needle and thread through a bead on the opposite side of the circle. Again, insert the needle and thread through the crystal and then return it to the bead that you first came out. Go inside that one bead and return the needle and thread to the outside of the circle (figure k).

(figure k)
Add picots to a bead circle.

6. Bring the needle over to a bead in the circle that is between a picot. Come out of that bead and make a leaf (page 93). Make another leaf starting at the bead that was skipped before making the next picot.

(figure l)
Finished flower.

7. Leave a long enough tail of thread to use it to attach the flower to the bracelet, corset, and neckline. Make as many flowers as desired. The sample doll has thirty-one of these flowers on various places.

THE SHOES

It is easier to put the shoes on Golendrial before dressing her, because the skirt will not get in the way.

1. Trace two Shoe Top pattern pieces (page 116) onto the wrong side of the painted piece of cotton that you also used for the corset. Cut out the shapes.

2. Place the Shoe Top pieces onto a piece of water-soluble stabilizer with the right side of the shoe up, and pin them in place.

3. With the variegated or decorative thread in the upper threader of your machine and metallic thread in the bobbin, free-motion embroider along the inner edge of the shoe tops and down onto the shoe. As you get to the sides of the shoes, free-motion embroider the tendrils as shown. The tendrils are stitched only on the stabilizer, without fabric (figure m). Later, these will be hand sewn to the doll's legs.

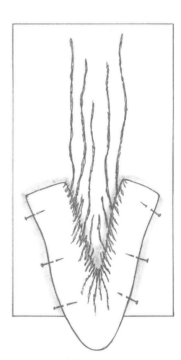

(figure m)
Sew tendrils along the shoe tops.

In free-motion sewing, it is important to lock your threads. What this means is when you leave the surface of the fabric and move onto the stabilizer, you must make sure you catch the threads as you sew up and down. If you do not, when the stabilizer is dissolved, the stitches will fall apart. I find it helpful to zigzag at least one way when I am sewing tendrils on the shoes or other items when working with free-motion machining. This locks the stitches together and prevents them from unraveling once the stabilizer is dissolved.

4. After you are finished with the free-motion sewing, place the shoe tops in lukewarm water to dissolve the stabilizer. Set the top of the shoes aside to dry.

5. While the shoe tops are drying, cut out two Shoe Sole pattern pieces (page 116) from the painted cotton. Using your fingers, fold the Soles in half lengthwise and crease each end of the folded edge. This gives you a guide for pinning the soles to the Shoe Tops.

6. When the Shoe Tops are dry, pin the back seam #1, right sides together, and sew them by machine.

7. Open up the seam allowances and finger-press the seam allowances open.

8. Pin the Sole of the shoe to the Shoe Top, right sides together, matching the crease in the soles, which you made earlier, to the back seam (#1) and the toe's center front (figure n). Starting at the back seam, sew all the way around. Do this carefully so you do not catch the tendrils you created along the top edge of the shoe. Turn right side out.

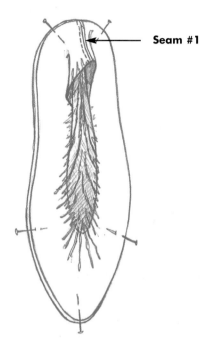

Seam #1

(figure n)
Sew the Shoe Sole to the Shoe Top, taking care not to catch the tendrils.

9. Place the shoes onto the feet of the doll. Because the shoes are larger than her feet, place some stuffing into the toes of the shoes. Fairies always wear pointy-toed shoes. This is so they can push the moss around on the ground when searching for crystals.

10. Hand sew the tendrils to the legs and add seed beads here and there along the tendrils. Add a few seed beads along the edge of the shoe tops.

THE FINISHING TOUCHES

1. To hide the seams at the doll's wrists, add beads. Thread up a beading needle with 1 yard (91 cm) of beading thread. Place a knot in the end.

2. Attach this thread to the inside of the wrist, over the seam. Thread up enough beads to wrap around her wrist. Close the circle by going into the first bead added. Tack along the strand of beads to her wrist.

3. Sew two more rows of seed beads around each wrist and weave them together to create the look of a three-row bracelet.

4. Hand sew some of the beaded flowers to the circle of beads around her wrist (figure o). Do the same with the other wrist.

(figure o)
Weave strands of beads for the bracelets.

5. For the skirt, sew the back seam of the silk crepe de Chine, right sides together.

6. Pin the top edges of the organza skirt to the silk skirt, with the wrong side of the organza against the right side of the silk. By machine, sew a gathering stitch along the pinned top edge. Slip the skirts onto the doll's body and pull the threads to fit snugly. Hand sew the top of the skirt directly to the body.

7. Place the corset over the skirt and bodice. Pin the back opening by overlapping the back's finished edge on top of the unfinished edge. Hand sew the back closed.

8. To give a nice neckline to the bodice, sew some crystal-colored seed beads around her neck and down onto the bodice. Add the beaded flowers along the top edge of the bodice and another one at the center of the neck (figure p).

(figure p)
For the beaded neckpiece, sew the beads directly to the doll.

THE HEADPIECE AND HAIR

1. Using three strands of the decorative YLI or Kreinik threads, braid a headpiece. A lucet was used to create Golendrial's braid. A simple braid can be done by hand.

2. Measure the head as you make the braid so that it will wrap around the top of the doll's head. When you have the proper length, secure the end of the braid with a knot. With an overhand knot, tie the two ends of the braid together to form a circle. Leave the ends long and attach beads and free-motion leaves to the ends.

3. Hand sew more of the flowered beads along the front of the headpiece, and a few at each side. The back will not show that much due to the doll's hair.

4. The hair used on the sample doll is an oblong piece of Tibetan goat hair. Cut a piece from the hide side of the hair. You will need a piece 3" wide by 5" long (7.6 × 12.7 cm).

To cut the goat hair, make a snip in the hide, then tear the rest of the way. This keeps the hairs from falling out.

5. To give a nice hairline, pin the hide to the head with the hair side down on the doll's forehead. The length of the hide will be towards the front of her face (figure q).

(figure q)
Sew the Tibetan goat hair to the head.

6. Hand sew this front edge in place with a strong needle and thread. Flip the skin back and pin the skin behind the doll's ears and at each side of the back of her head. Hand sew it in place. If any of the hide shows, tuck it under and hand sew it in place.

7. Place the headpiece on the doll's head (figure r) and hand sew (tack) it in at least three places to keep it from falling off.

(figure r)
Attach the hair before positioning the headpiece.

THE WINGS

1. Trace the Wing pattern (page 117) onto a piece of water-soluble stabilizer, leaving room on the sheet to trace another wing. Fold over the other (untraced) side of the stabilizer on top of the traced wing. Trace on this side. This gives you a right and left wing.

2. Pin the stabilizer with tracings onto a piece of cream-colored organza.

3. Place a decorative thread in the upper threader of the sewing machine and metallic thread in the bobbin. Machine sew, using a straight stitch, around the outline of the wings and along the veins.

4. If you have an embroidery presser foot that has a hole in the front (sometimes called a cording foot), put it on the sewing machine. (For a Bernina sewing machine, this foot is #6.) Feed the beading wire into the hole of the foot. Set the machine for a zigzag stitch, lower the width to 2 (slightly narrow) and the length to 1 (very short).

6. Zigzag the wire to the right side of the wings where marked on the pattern piece(s). When you finish with each line, cut the wire, leaving about 1" (2.5 cm) free at each end.

7. Carefully cut out the wings, making sure you do not cut into the stitches, especially where the wire is attached. Place the wings into lukewarm water to dissolve the stabilizer. Let the wings air dry.

(figure s)
Stabilize the organza to stitch the wings.

8. Once the wings are dry, paint them with Lumiere paints. The sample doll wings were colored with halo violet gold, pearlescent violet, and sunset gold. Start with the darker colors close to the center edges of the wings (pearlescent violet), then apply the halo violet gold and, on the outer edges, the sunset gold.

9. Collect the gold charlottes (or other size 11/12 seed beads) and crystals. Slip three charlottes or seed beads onto a wire at the end of a wing, then a crystal, and finally two seed beads. Cut the wire and pinch under the end to keep the beads in place. Do this to all of the wires on the wings.

10. Pin the wings to the back of Golendrial and hand sew them in place using matching thread. A few couching stitches will secure the wings to her back. To cover your stitches on her back, you can add beaded flowers. The wires in the wings will keep them steady.

Michelle Meinhold is known for her wonderful beadwork. For this sample, she attached seed beads with a peyote bead stitch. It is also easy to follow a cross-stitch pattern to create this type of design.

Kathryn Thompson used a soldering iron and layers of nylon organza to create her whimsical wings. The organza was layered, machine stitched in a free-motion design, and then she used the soldering iron to burn away areas to expose light and the design.

THE PURSE

All fairies need a wee special purse to carry their crystals, threads for bird nests, and a few berries to snack on. It must have a few beads dangling from it and some small bells. The bells are special ones that only other fairies can hear. When you are in the woods, you must let your friends know that you are approaching. Otherwise, you may miss them. Fairies are shy and do not want to be seen by humans.

1. Using tissue paper or pattern paper, trace the Purse pattern (page 116) to make a template. Cut a piece of velvet from this template. Thread a hand sewing needle with an 18" (45.7 cm) length of thread. Place a knot in the end of the thread.

(figure t)
Draw up the edges of a circle for the purse.

2. Attach the thread to the inside top of the circle of velvet and hand sew a gathering stitch completely around the edge (figure t). Pull the thread to close the top of the purse. Do not close the top too tightly. Goldendrial needs enough of an opening to drop her goodies inside. Anchor the thread with several small stitches and then cut off the ends of the threads.

3. Create another braid for the handle of the purse using the same threads you used for the headpiece. Leave about 2" (5 cm) of thread free on both ends of the braid. Place beads and some small bells on the ends. Hand sew the handle to the purse.

4. Thread a beading needle with 12" (30.5 cm) of beading thread. Place a knot in the end. Attach this to the bottom of the doll's purse, on the outside. Pick up a decorative bead, a larger drop-shaped bead, and a small drop-shaped bead. Skipping the small drop-shaped bead, go back through the larger bead and the decorative bead and into the bottom of the purse. Anchor the thread with several small stitches and cut off the thread end.

If you want, hand sew some beads on Golendrial's ear lobes for earrings. Place some crystals and threads in her purse and she's ready. I wouldn't put any berries in right now. They may spoil.

GALLERY

EO THE ARBER

Melinda Small Paterson

The artist writes:

Eo needed a nose, ears, and feet that were larger than what the pattern provided. For her green woodsy costume, I laid a combination of fabrics around her and chose the darkest for her tunic, a textured one for the hat and shoes, and a shimmery one for the blouse. Pieces were pinned in place and then trimmed or gathered to fit. The blouse scraps were just enough to wrap her neck, front, and arms. Each pant leg is a tube equal to her hip measurement and gathered below her knee. Her tunic is a rectangle with a neck hole in the center and a cut down the front. A felt lining, cuffs, and trims were sewn while it was flat, then the sides were sewn closed and the waist gathered.

For the felt soles of her shoes, I traced around her foot, then sewed a triangle at the heel and a long triangle for the toe. The hat is a longer slim triangle with another tapering piece for the brim and side dangles. Stuffing went into the toes and hat, with gathering stitches to make them curl.

The wings started with Mylar pinned to cardboard over my drawing. Clear acrylic medium was brushed on to secure layers of netting and lace bits. Black lines were machine sewn and florist wire was satin stitched on the top edge using a cording foot. Then they were cut out along the outline.

When I'd sewn all I could by machine, the clothes were sewn onto the doll. The tunic was sewn last. An opening was cut in the neck back to fit around the wings, then sewn shut.

CHRYSTABELLA

Adele Sciortino

The artist writes:

Dried skeleton leaves painted gold started the design for the dress Chrystabella is wearing. These were hand sewn around the neck. The bust area is adorned in small pheasant feathers. The main part of the dress is made with silk crinkle fabric that was then tucked and adorned with pearl-like beads. The over-skirt was made from the same crinkle silk and overlaid with imported beaded fabric. Pheasant tail feathers were added to the sleeves, and wild berries were attached to pick up the color of the hair.

The wings started with a wire base and iridescent organza. After they were sewn and trimmed, the edges were tipped in gold glass glitter and covered in two different colors of micro beads.

Two-part clay was used to make the shoes. After the clay air dried, they were painted in gold and silver. More crystals and gold glass glitter were added to give them that fairylike magic.

Her final accessory was a scepter made from two-part clay. Swarovski crystals give the scepter its sparkle. The top crystal bauble is decorated with two-color microbeads, lighting the long Canadian winter nights.

UMQHAGI

Sue Farmer

The artist writes:

Umqhagi is a Xhosa word for rooster. This was the inspiration for the costume. Generally, I scribble a thumbnail sketch of the costume as a starting point, then I let the fabric dictate what the finished design will be. I tend to drape the fabric on the body or use paper towels to mock up the patterns. This is simpler than taking measurements and flat drafting (For more on draping techniques, see page 69.)

Living in Africa since childhood has strongly influenced my taste in color and costume. Sunrise and sunsets are spectacular here, and the connection with heat, dust, and the early morning cock-crow became the inspiration for the wings and overall coloring.

A rich Batavian print combined with a silk pongee and coarse black tulle was the starting point. The silk needed to be dyed so the colors were painted on with Dye-Na-Flow dyes while wet. Next came antique pleating, which is simple to do and creates a very attractive texture. To keep the soft look, the edges were frayed with a pin.

The bodice was originally intended to be a corset/bib, but the stiff look of the breastplate seemed a more interesting way to go—and led to the topstitched peplum used to disguise the top edge of the skirt.

The length of the neck was perfect for the gold-coiled look, a feature of African women, and a rooster-tail effect made rather interesting wings. Simple bead embellishment connected the print sections. The ankle and wrist beads were used to tie the black stitching of the wings into the rest of the design.

Head dressing in South Africa tends to be a simple bandanna or doek tied at the base of the neck. This was combined with West African drapes and "butterfly ends" for a prettier look.

Ꝯake a Ꝯish

Darcy Balcomb

The artist writes:

The first challenge was creating movement, as if in flight. The doll was positioned this way, painted with gesso, sanded, and then rubbed with flesh-colored paint. A final coat of spray shellac was used for gloss and dimension. The stand was padded and covered with pieces of vintage sari and silk.

The next challenge was to create clothing that would convey texture and movement. I like to work with scraps. Starting with the upper body, remnants from a recent knitting project were attached. Tan-colored tulle was sewn in place as an overskin and brushed with water-diluted glue. This technique left much of her flesh showing while still providing a top for her dress.

Various scraps of fabric were heat "distressed" and, along with some floral elements and fibers, sewn individually around the waist. Her hair is also made from more than one hundred hand-painted pieces of "distressed" fabric.

The wings are embellished leaves from a silk magnolia tree. She has a glass wand and a whimsical crown made from three hand-knitted triangles. Instead of using seed beads for embellishment, I sprinkled the doll with mini no-sew beads at the base and on the bodice and arms. Rhinestones add further sparkle. She also holds secrets and symbols, some of which reside on the scrolls in her purse.

MEADOWSWEET

Sandra Johns

The artist writes:

Looking through my stash, I found a felted hat I had made years ago. It had leaf shapes and touches of flowers in it. At the time, I loved the shapes, but didn't know what to do with it. Knowing it would make wonderful fairy wings, I took the hat apart. I then quilted it and figured out what shapes I wanted for the wings. They couldn't be exactly the same on both sides, so I didn't even try. After the shape was cut out, I machine stitched a wire edge for strength and control.

There was enough felt left over to make the slippers. I used paper to draw the sole of the foot. I used this pattern to cut out the felt. This was pinned to her feet and hand sewn directly to the foot. The leaf-shaped felt was used for the shoe top and hand sewn in place. This gave her slippers a fly-away look. A little orange felt flower created the buckle and was attached using seed beads.

Scarves were used for the leggings and provided a pleasing layering of color. Yarns were used to tie them just below and just above the knee. The overskirt is silk with burned edges. The bodice has free-motion machined edging.

Her fairy coat is created in two sections, which allow her wings to fly freely. The ends of the coat have felted leaves hand-sewn on and embellished with seed beads. Extra leaves complete the headpiece. The traveling bag is made from handmade felt. It holds the other half of her coat. She's now ready to go into the wintry forest for an evening fairy gathering.

MELBA

Pam Gonzalez

The artist writes:

The large autumn maple leaves in my backyard in the Pacific Northwest inspired the creation of Melba, the Woodland Fairy. I preserved the leaves using glycerin and then free-motion embroidered on them to show off the leaves' veins. I modified the pattern by giving the doll long toes and only four long fingers. I also modified the pattern by bending her legs so she might sit on her log in the forest.

I began costuming Melba by hand beading the pink and orange spots on her batik fabric body with seed beads. I love working with bright colors. I hand-painted cheesecloth, Venice lace, and polyester crinkle cloth using Jacquard's Dye-Na-Flow and Lumiere paints. I draped the fabric directly on the body to form the clothing. I wrapped cheesecloth around her legs for pantaloons and across her bodice. I also used pink- and copper-colored Angelina fibers fused between the cheesecloth. Her skirt features layers of hand-gathered cheesecloth and crinkle cloth with burnt edges and Venice lace. I added more beads to the skirt to give her a little more sparkle. Velvet leaves, acorns, and miniature pinecones from my yard provide the final embellishments. Melba's namesake is my grandmother who had a passion for gardening.

PATTERNS

MODEL DOLL

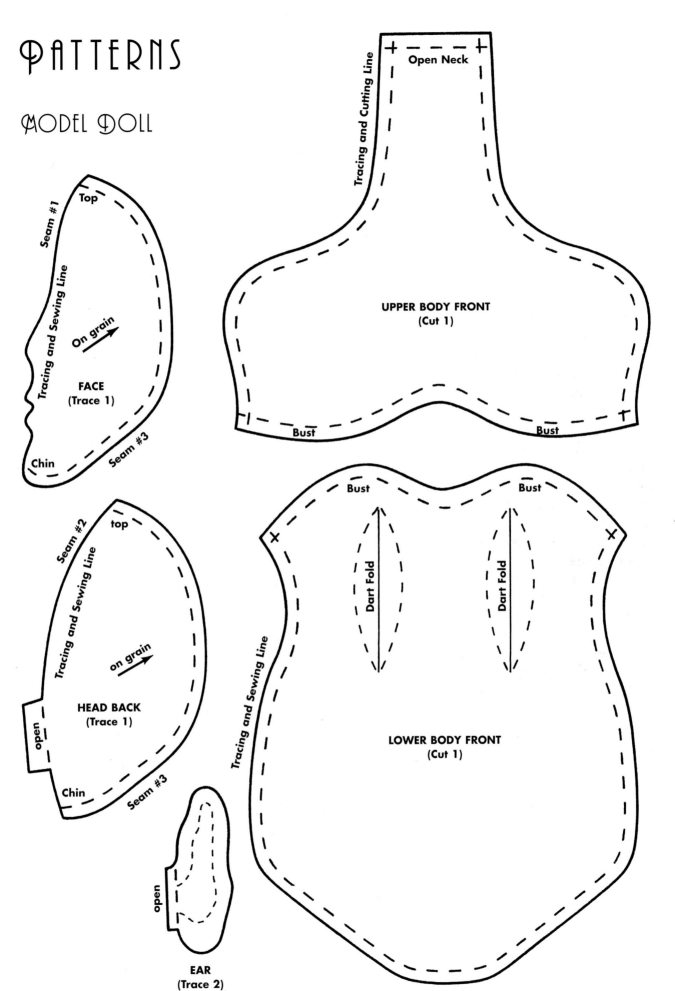

Open Neck

Tracing and Cutting Line

UPPER BODY FRONT
(Cut 1)

Bust   **Bust**

Seam #1   Top

Tracing and Sewing Line

On grain

FACE
(Trace 1)

Chin   Seam #3

Bust   **Bust**

Dart Fold   Dart Fold

Seam #2   top

Tracing and Sewing Line

on grain

HEAD BACK
(Trace 1)

open

Tracing and Sewing Line

Chin   Seam #3

LOWER BODY FRONT
(Cut 1)

open

EAR
(Trace 2)

Open Neck

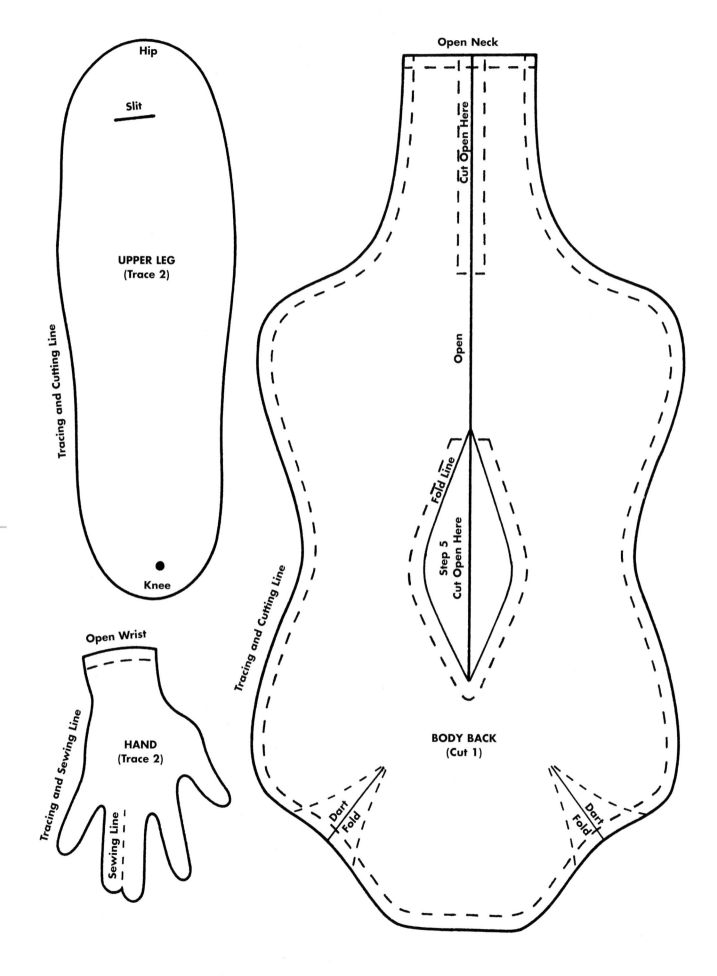

Hip

Slit

UPPER LEG
(Trace 2)

Tracing and Cutting Line

Knee

Open Neck

Cut Open Here

Open

Fold Line

Step 5
Cut Open Here

Tracing and Cutting Line

BODY BACK
(Cut 1)

Dart

Fold

Dart

Fold

Open Wrist

Tracing and Sewing Line

HAND
(Trace 2)

Sewing Line

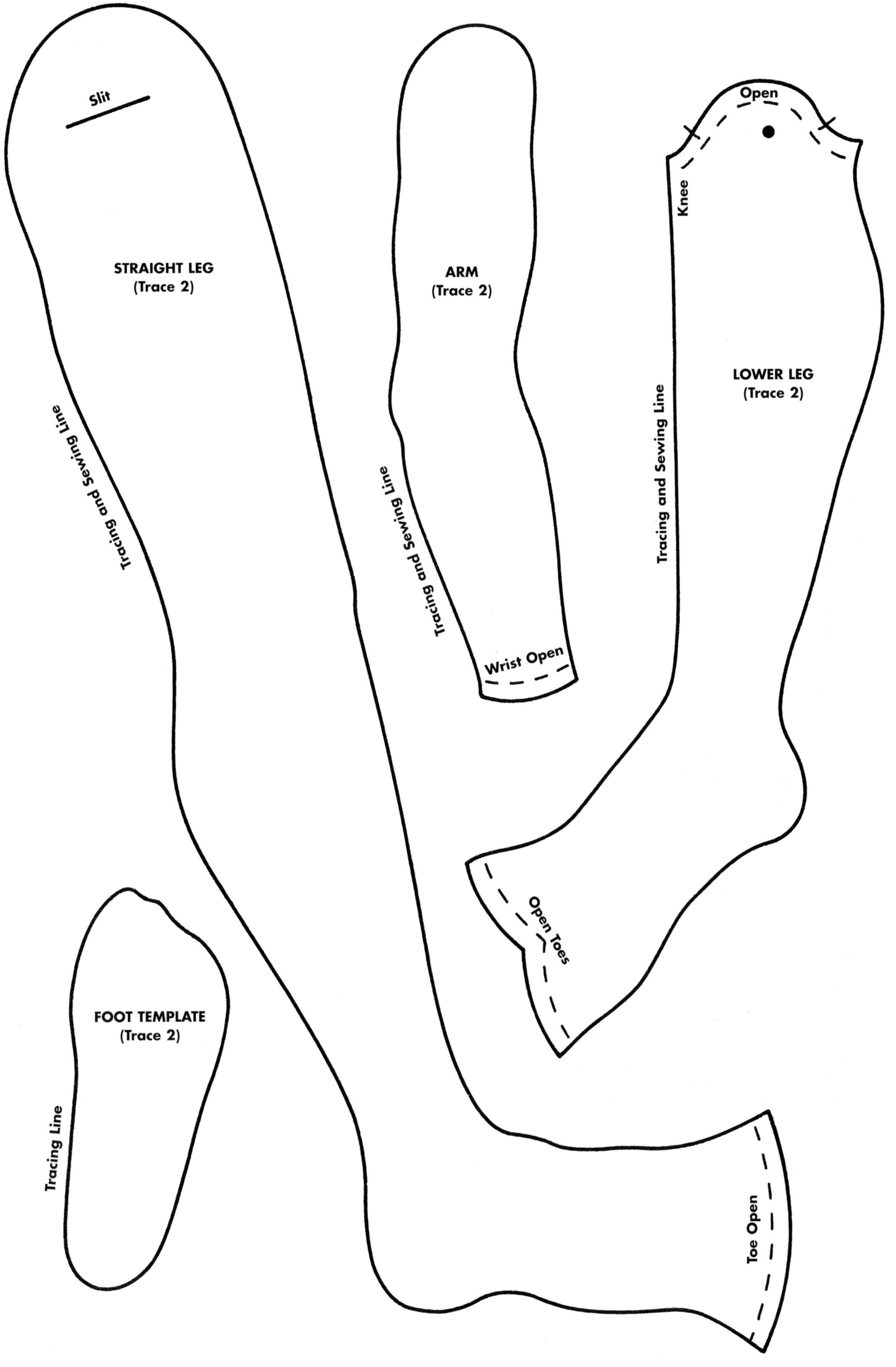

Slit

STRAIGHT LEG
(Trace 2)

Tracing and Sewing Line

ARM
(Trace 2)

Tracing and Sewing Line

Wrist Open

Open

Knee

LOWER LEG
(Trace 2)

Tracing and Sewing Line

Open Toes

FOOT TEMPLATE
(Trace 2)

Tracing Line

Toe Open

HELEN'S SUIT

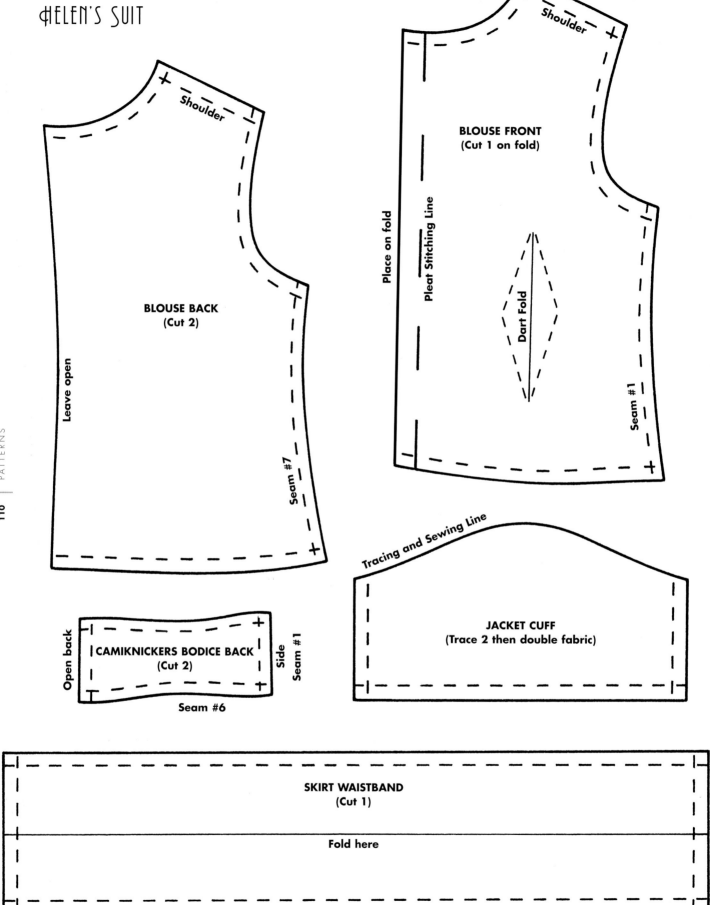

BLOUSE BACK
(Cut 2)

Shoulder

Leave open

Seam #7

BLOUSE FRONT
(Cut 1 on fold)

Shoulder

Place on fold

Pleat Stitching Line

Dart Fold

Seam #1

CAMIKNICKERS BODICE BACK
(Cut 2)

Open back

Side
Seam #1

Seam #6

Tracing and Sewing Line

JACKET CUFF
(Trace 2 then double fabric)

SKIRT WAISTBAND
(Cut 1)

Fold here

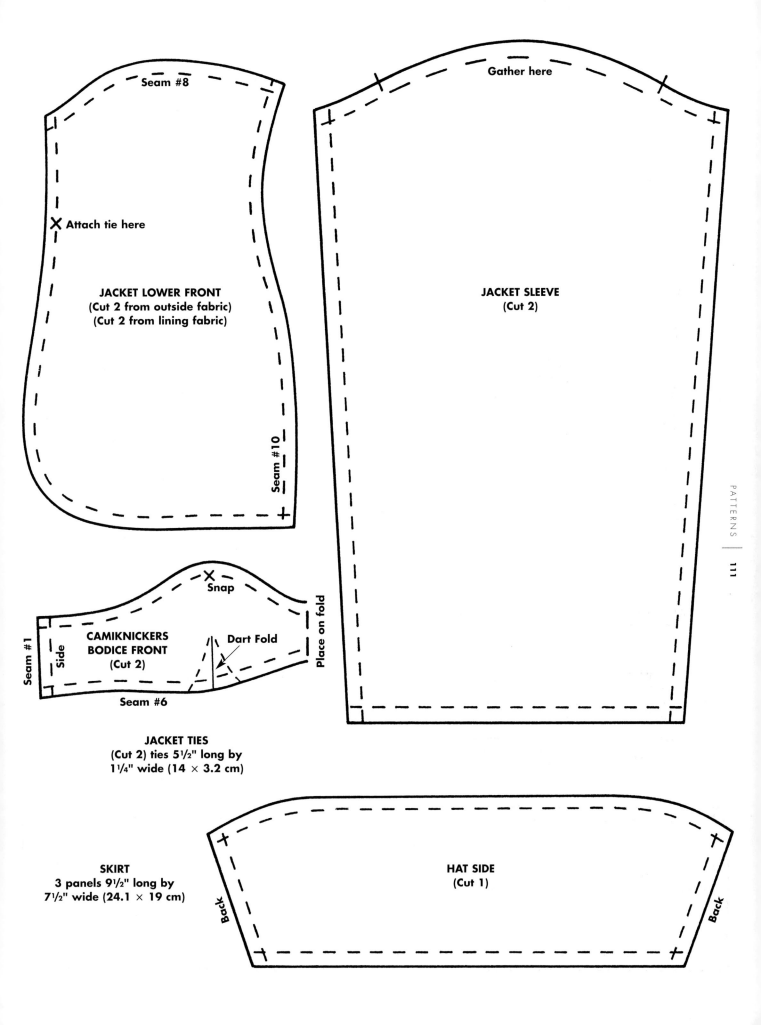

Seam #8

JACKET LOWER FRONT
(Cut 2 from outside fabric)
(Cut 2 from lining fabric)

X Attach tie here

Seam #10

JACKET SLEEVE
(Cut 2)

Gather here

Place on fold

CAMIKNICKERS
BODICE FRONT
(Cut 2)

X
Snap

Dart Fold

Seam #1

Side

Seam #6

JACKET TIES
(Cut 2) ties 5½" long by
1¼" wide (14 × 3.2 cm)

SKIRT
3 panels 9½" long by
7½" wide (24.1 × 19 cm)

HAT SIDE
(Cut 1)

Back

Back

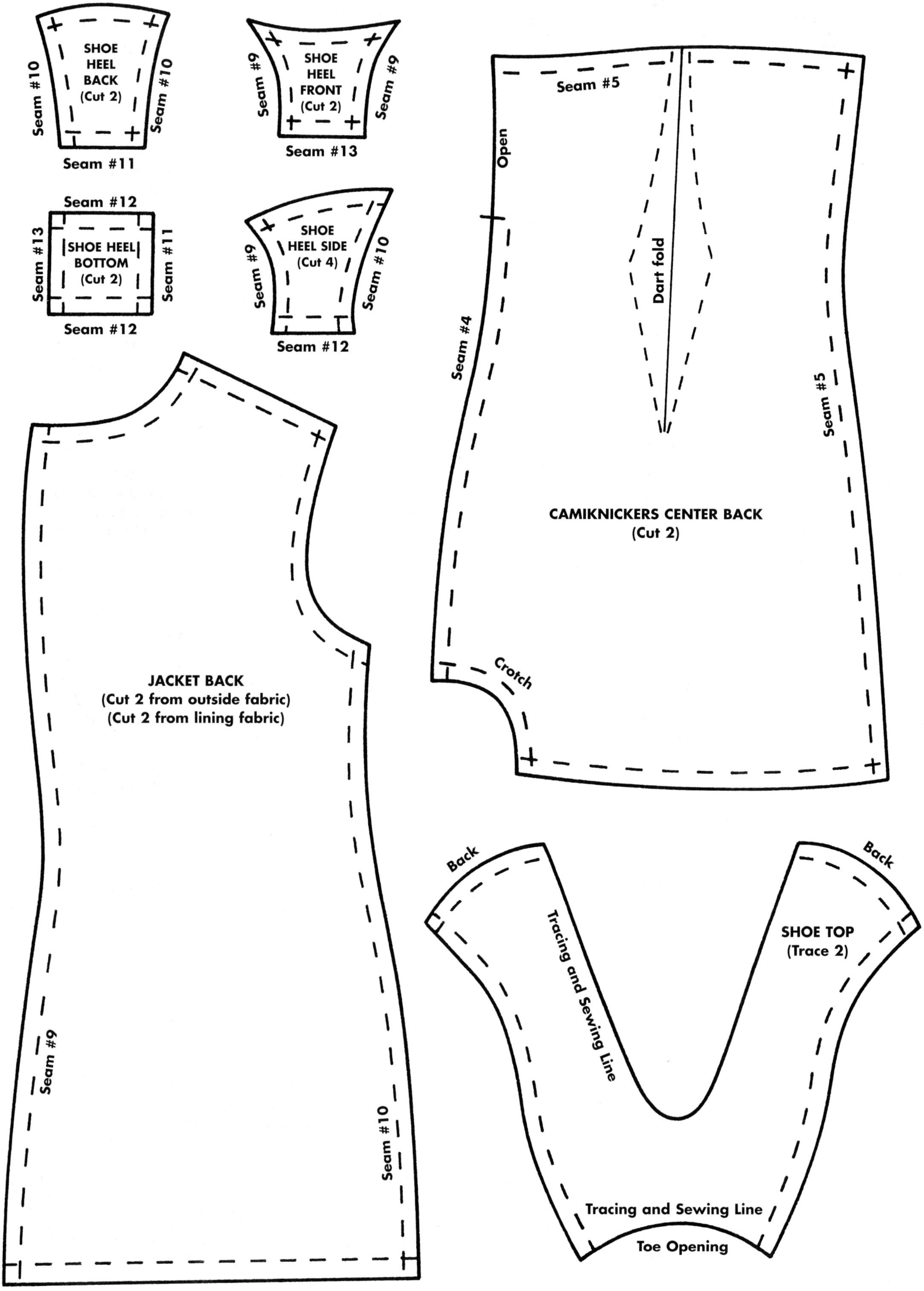

SHOE HEEL BACK
(Cut 2)

Seam #10
Seam #10
Seam #11

SHOE HEEL FRONT
(Cut 2)

Seam #9
Seam #9
Seam #13

SHOE HEEL BOTTOM
(Cut 2)

Seam #12
Seam #13
Seam #11
Seam #12

SHOE HEEL SIDE
(Cut 4)

Seam #9
Seam #10
Seam #12

CAMIKNICKERS CENTER BACK
(Cut 2)

Seam #5
Open
Seam #4
Dart fold
Seam #5
Crotch

JACKET BACK
(Cut 2 from outside fabric)
(Cut 2 from lining fabric)

Seam #9
Seam #10

Back
Tracing and Sewing Line
Back
SHOE TOP
(Trace 2)
Tracing and Sewing Line
Toe Opening

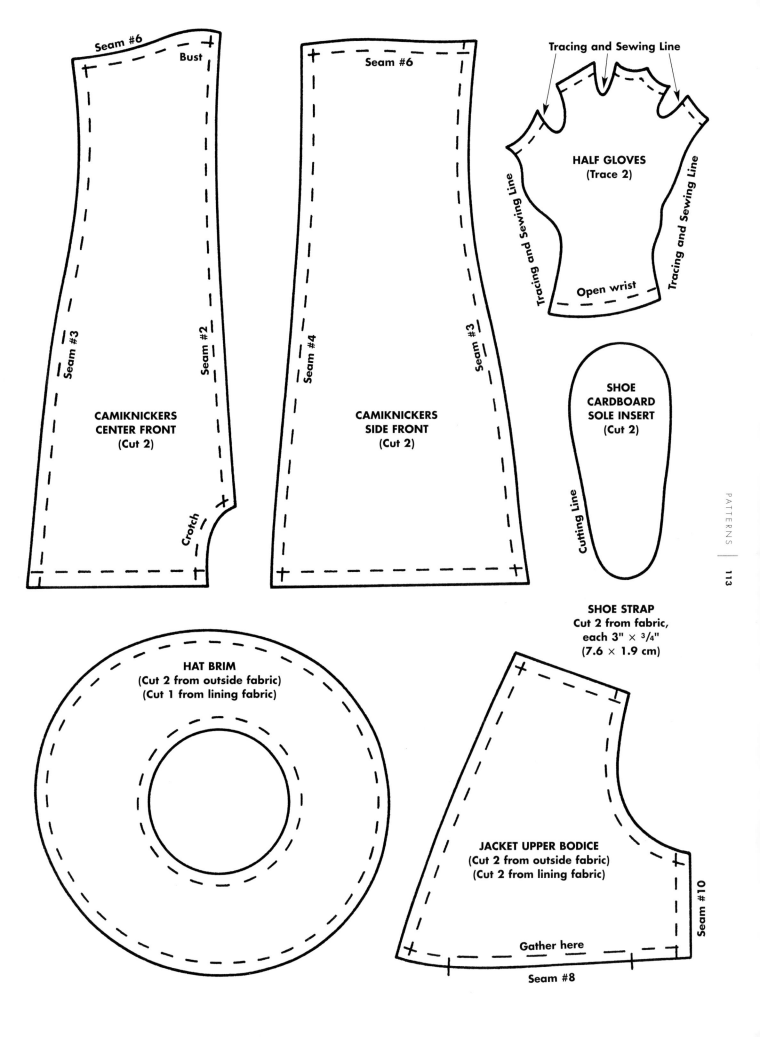

Seam #6

Bust

CAMIKNICKERS
CENTER FRONT
(Cut 2)

Seam #3

Seam #2

Crotch

Seam #6

CAMIKNICKERS
SIDE FRONT
(Cut 2)

Seam #4

Seam #3

Tracing and Sewing Line

HALF GLOVES
(Trace 2)

Tracing and Sewing Line

Tracing and Sewing Line

Open wrist

SHOE
CARDBOARD
SOLE INSERT
(Cut 2)

Cutting Line

SHOE STRAP
Cut 2 from fabric,
each 3" × 3/4"
(7.6 × 1.9 cm)

HAT BRIM
(Cut 2 from outside fabric)
(Cut 1 from lining fabric)

JACKET UPPER BODICE
(Cut 2 from outside fabric)
(Cut 2 from lining fabric)

Seam #10

Gather here

Seam #8

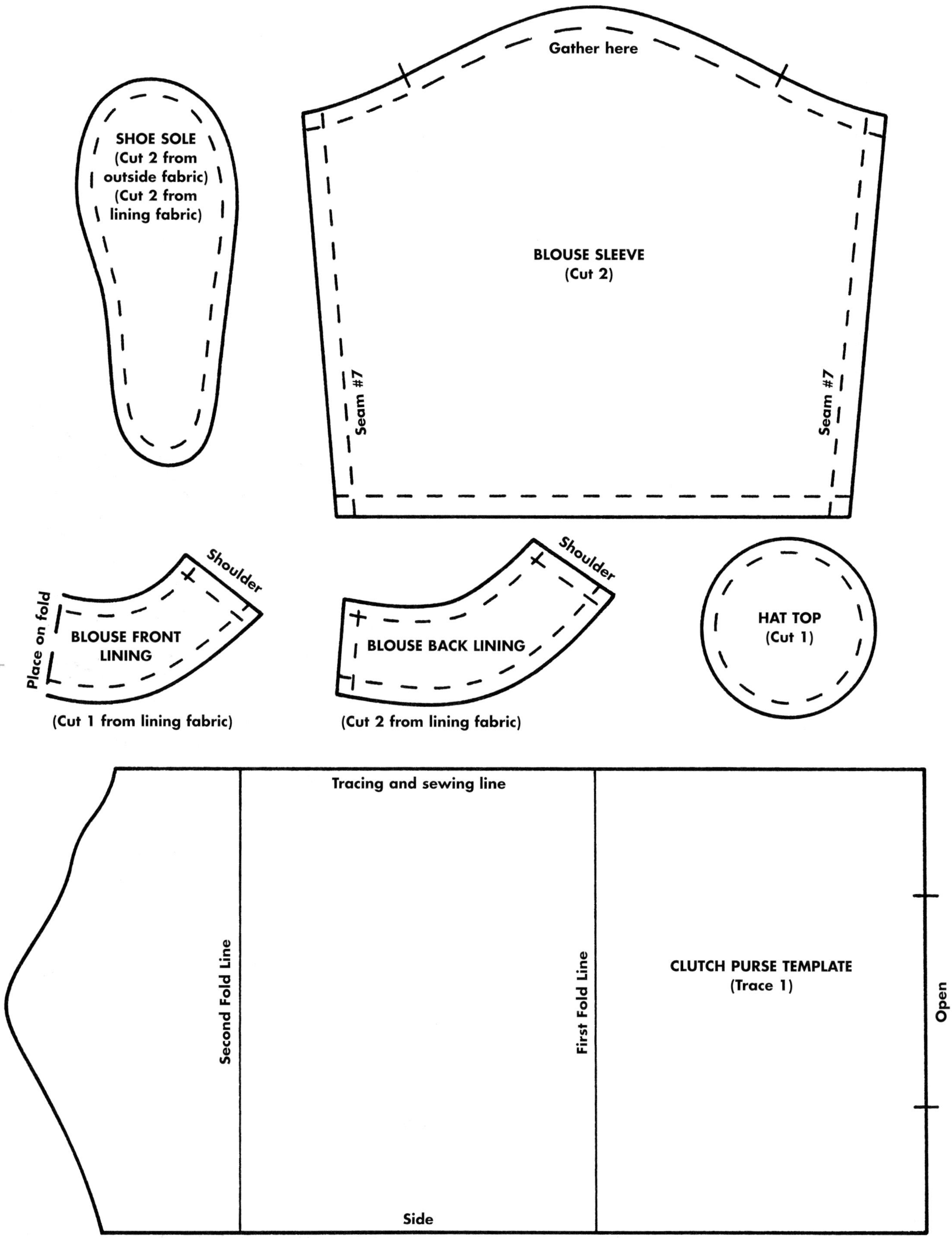

SHOE SOLE
(Cut 2 from outside fabric)
(Cut 2 from lining fabric)

BLOUSE SLEEVE
(Cut 2)

Gather here

Seam #7

Seam #7

Place on fold

Shoulder

BLOUSE FRONT LINING

(Cut 1 from lining fabric)

Shoulder

BLOUSE BACK LINING

(Cut 2 from lining fabric)

HAT TOP
(Cut 1)

Tracing and sewing line

Second Fold Line

First Fold Line

CLUTCH PURSE TEMPLATE
(Trace 1)

Open

Side

ELIZABETHE'S ACCESSORIES

PAINTED FIGURE FOR PHOTO TRANSFER

GENERAL SHAPE
For sleeves, purses, embellishments

Tracing and Sewing Line

Tracing Lines

LEAF
(Trace 1)

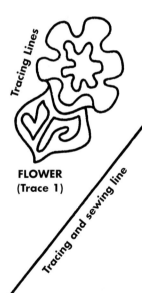

Tracing Lines

FLOWER
(Trace 1)

BOOT TOP
(Trace 4)

Tracing and Sewing Line

Seam #1

Tracing and sewing line

SKIRT EDGING

GOLENDRIAL'S FAIRY OUTFIT

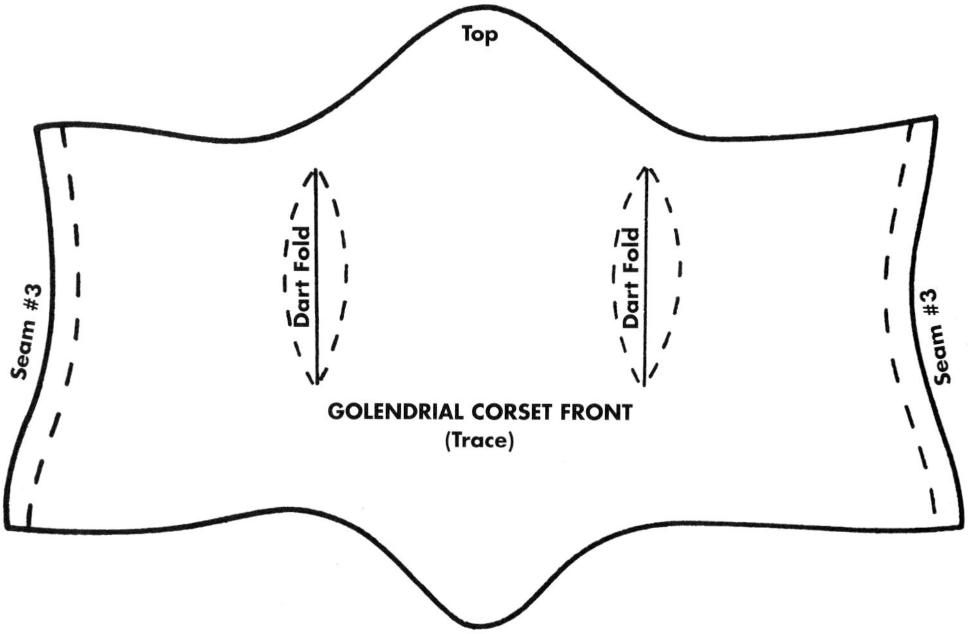

Top

Seam #3

Dart Fold

Dart Fold

Seam #3

GOLENDRIAL CORSET FRONT
(Trace)

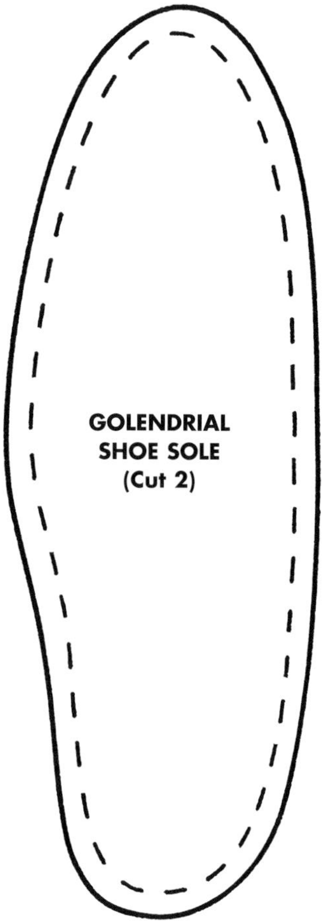

GOLENDRIAL
SHOE SOLE
(Cut 2)

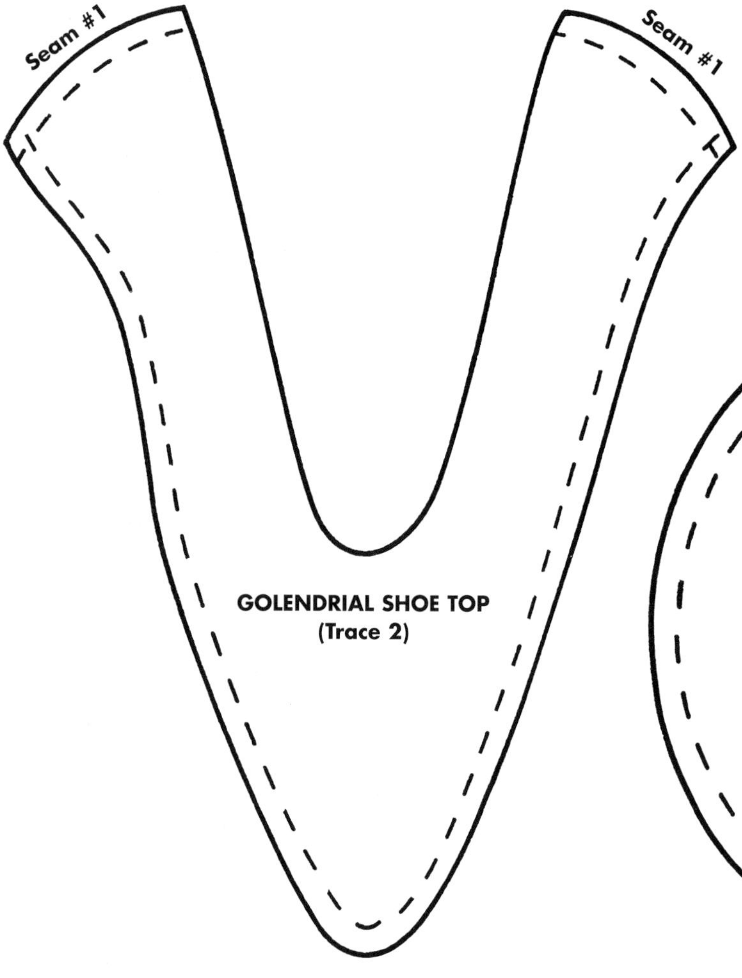

Seam #1

Seam #1

GOLENDRIAL SHOE TOP
(Trace 2)

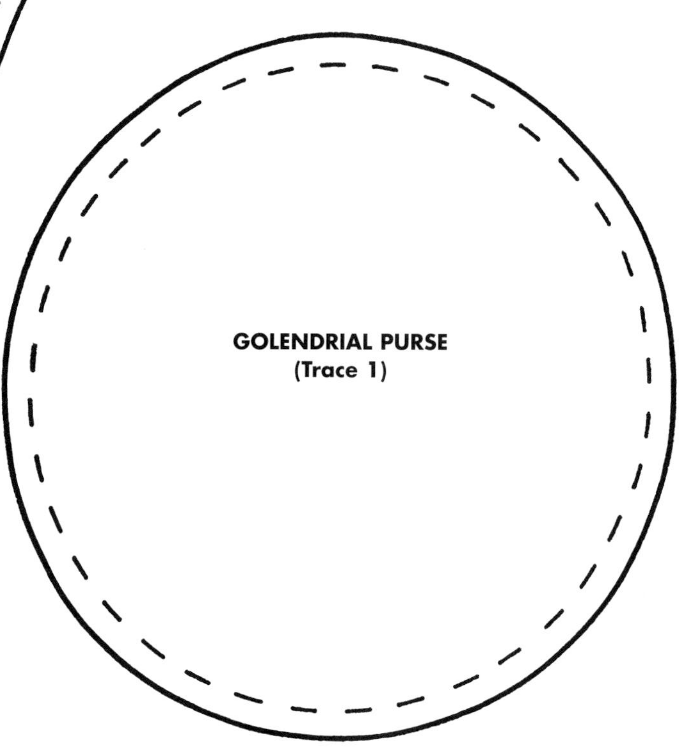

GOLENDRIAL PURSE
(Trace 1)

BAUBLE
(Trace 11)

FLOWER
(Trace 7)

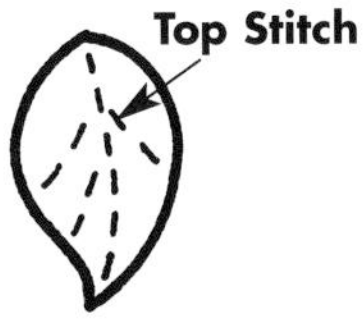

Top Stitch

LEAF
(Trace 9)

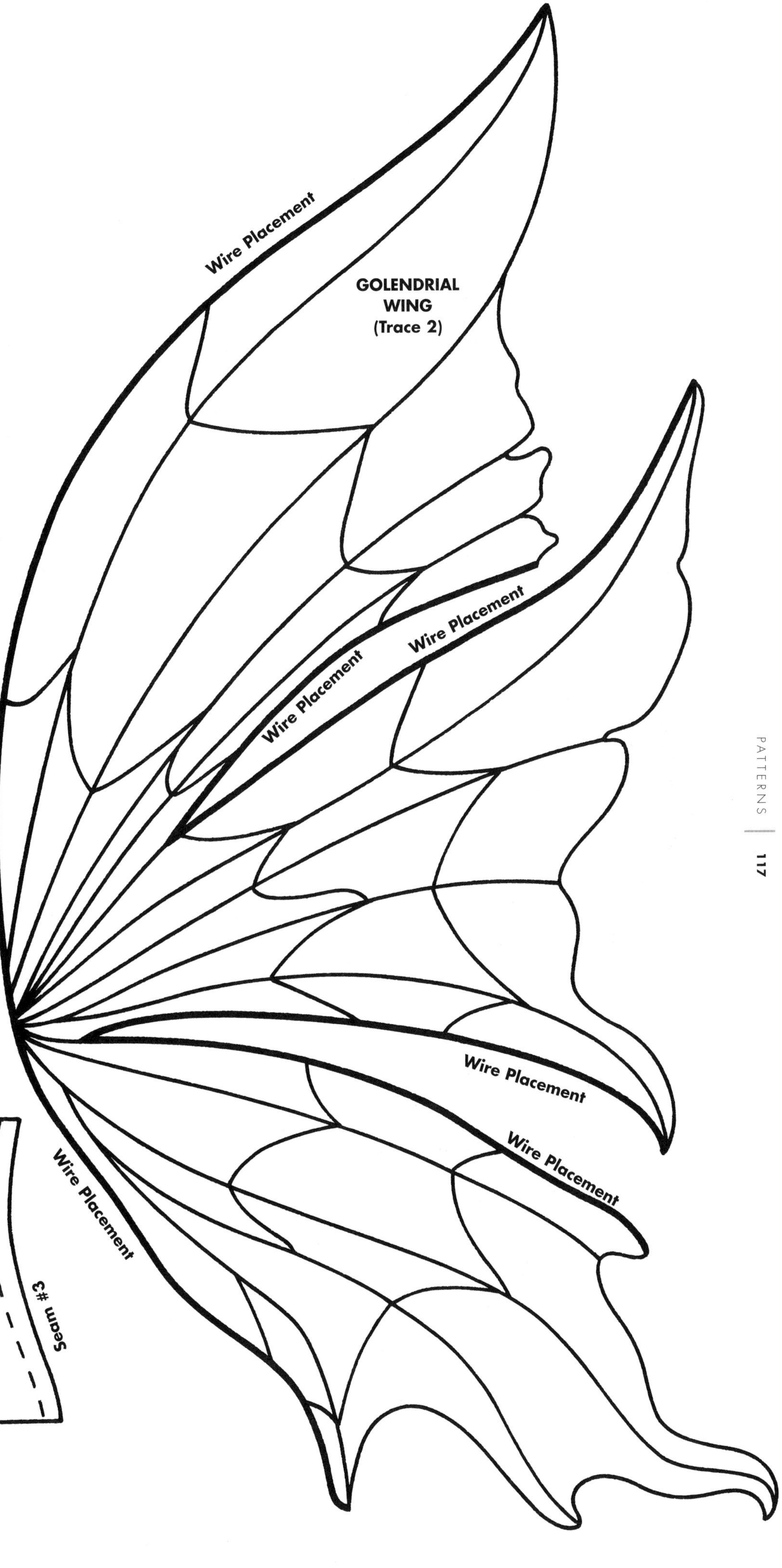

Wire Placement

GOLENDRIAL
WING
(Trace 2)

Wire Placement

Wire Placement

Wire Placement

Wire Placement

Wire Placement

Wire Placement

Back

Dart Fold

Seam #3

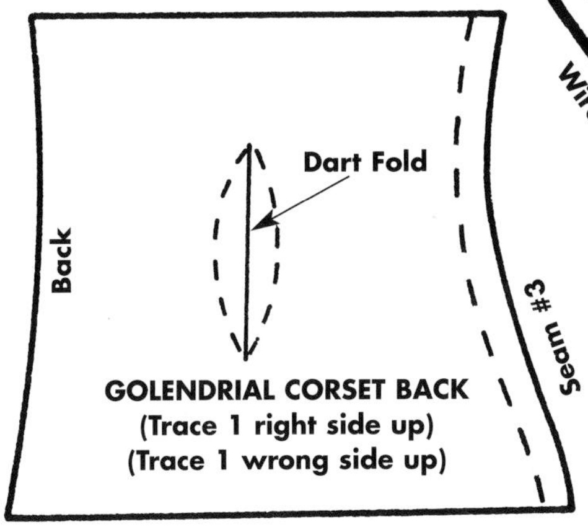

GOLENDRIAL CORSET BACK
(Trace 1 right side up)
(Trace 1 wrong side up)

APPENDIX BEAD EMBROIDERY STITCHES

BACK STITCH

1. Place a knot in the thread and come up from the underside of the fabric (A).

2. String on nine beads. Hold the thread taut with your thumb. Needle down through the fabric and come up in between the sixth and seventh beads (B).

3. Go through the holes in the seventh and eighth beads (C). Insert the needle down into the fabric (D).

4. Move over to the fourth bead and come up and through the fourth bead (E). Go through the fifth, sixth, and seventh beads (F).

5. Put the needle back into the fabric and bring it over to the second bead (G). Come up and go through the second through ninth beads (H).

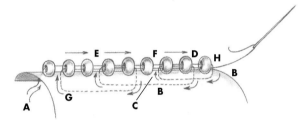

6. Continue repeating steps 2–5 until you have laid down the length of beads that you want.

Back stitch beading

Beaded Fringe Option 1

1. This is not really an embroidery stitch, but if you laid it down flat on the surface of a garment and couched it, it would be. Anchor the thread and come out from the edge of the fabric (A).

2. Add several size 11/12 seed beads, a few size 6/7 seed beads, an accent bead (such as a crystal) and finally a drop bead (B).

3. Skip the drop bead and go back up through the beads and into the fabric (C and A).

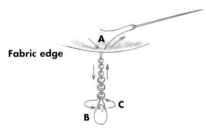

**Option 1
Beaded fringe**

Beaded Fringe Option 2

1. Thread up several size 6/7 beads then 3–5 (or as many you want) size 11/12 seed beads, a drop bead, and an equal number of size 11/12 seed beads.

2. Go through the size 6/7 beads and into the fabric (D).

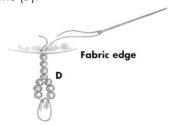

**Option 2
Beaded fringe**

Ladder Stitch

1. Stitch down from the front of the piece (A).

2. Hiding the thread, go into and out at the seam (B).

3. Run the needle under the fabric for a bit, and then take the needle out through the fabric (C).

4. Push the needle into the fabric at (D).

5. Run the needle under the fabric for a bit and take the needle out through the fabric at (E).

6. Continue this process until the seam is finished.

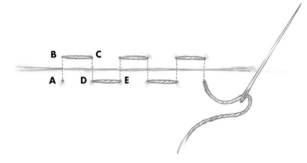

Ladder stitch

Note: Illustration details stitching on the underside of the seam.

Stacks

1. Stacks can be made with two beads, or as many as you would like to add. They add dimension to the surface you are working on. Anchor the thread and come up from the underside of the fabric (A). Pick up a size 6/7 bead and then a size 11/12 seed bead. Skip the size 11/12 seed bead. Go down through the size 6/7 bead and into the fabric at A.

2. On the underside of the fabric, move along to the desired location of the next stack (B). Insert the needle through the fabric and then repeat step 1.

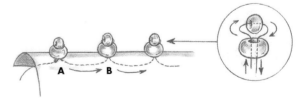

Stack stitch

RESOURCES

UNITED STATES

Caravan Beads and Fibers
915 Forest Avenue
Portland, ME 04103
207-761-2503
www.caravanbeads.com
Complete line of beads, retail and wholesale

Cloth Doll Connection
www.clothdollconnection.com
Online doll-making classes, links, and a calendar of events

Dollmakers Journey
www.DollmakersJourney.com
Books, patterns, supplies for the contemporary doll artist

Doll Heaven
Lisa Risler
2590 FM 356
Trinity, TX 75862
936-594-6703
www.lisasheaven.com
lisasheaven@cebridge.net
All your doll supply needs: mohair, online classes, paints, patterns

Joggles, Inc.
www.joggles.com
Books, fabrics, mohair, and other fibers; patterns

Meinke Toy
PMB #411
55 E. Long Lake Road
Troy, MI 48085
www.meinketoy.com
info@meinketoy.com
Books, Meadowbrook Industries Angelina Heat-Bondable Fiber, threads, stabilizers

PMC Designs
9019 Stargaze Avenue
San Diego, CA 92129
858-484-5118
www.pmcdesigns.com
patti@pmcdesigns.com
Classes, newsletters, one-of-a-kind dolls, patterns, tools (including the Itsy Bitsy Turner)

Quilting Arts Magazine
Cloth Paper Scissors
Quilting Arts Store
P.O. Box 685
Stow, MA 01775
www.quiltingarts.com
Books, magazines, Meadowbrook Industries Angelina Heat-Bondable Fiber, silk, stabilizers

Robertsons' Enterprises
Box 357
Dolores, CO 81323
970-882-3389
Catalog of hard-to-find cloth doll supplies (send $3 for the catalog)

Rupert Gibbon & Spider
P.O. Box 425
Healdsburg, CA 95448
1-800-442-0455
www.jacquardproducts.com
Jacquard products: Dye-NA-Flow, Lumiere, and textile paints

Terry Medaris Art Stamps
www.terrymedarisartstamps.com
Beautiful images to use on clothing and doll bodies, greeting cards, prints, stamps, workshops

Textura Trading Company
Eastworks Building
116 Pleasant Street, Suite 3409
Easthampton, MA 01027
877–TEXTURA
www.texturatrading.com
Angelina Fiber

Tsukineko, Inc.
17640 NE 65th Street
Redmond, WA 98052
425-883-7733
www.tsukineko.com
Fantastix, stamp pads

CANADA

Opus Framing & Art Studio
www.opusframing.com
Books, Jacquard products, workshops

Bobbins 'n' Bears Studio
#108 561 Johnson Street
Victoria, BC V8W 1M2
www.bobbinsstudio.com
Beads, dyes and paints, fabrics, mohair, patterns, stabilizers

AUSTRALIA

Anne's Glory Box
60 Beaumont Street
Hamilton
NSW 2303
+61 2 4961 6016
www.annesglorybox.com.au
Beads, books, dyes and paints, fabrics, mohair, stabilizers

Things I Like
RSD 7A Mambray Creek
Via Port Pirie
South Australia 5540
www.thingsilike.net
thsilike@westnet.com.au
Patterns, fabrics, full line of supplies for cloth doll making

The Thread Studio
6 Smith Street
Perth
Western Australia 6000
+61 8 9227 1561
www.thethreadstudio.com
Books, online classes, paints, stabilizers, threads

Yadeno Fibre Craft
35 Lake Drive
Meringandan
Queensland 4352
+61 07 4696 9329
www.yadenofibrecraft.com.au

NEW ZEALAND

Elna Sewing and Jan's Patch
235 Moray Place
Box 5227
Dunedin
www.elna-janspatch.co.nz
Books, fabric, Meadowbrook Industries Angelina Heat-Bondable Fiber, paints, stabilizers, yarns, and wool

Zigzag Polymer Clay Supplies Ltd.
8 Cherry Place
Casebrook, Christchurch
+64 3 359 2989
www.2dye4.co.nz
Jacquard products, Prismacolor pencils, rubber stamps

UNITED KINGDOM

Art Van Go
1 Stevenage Road
Knebworth
Herts SG3 6AN
England
+44 01438 814946
www.artvango.co.uk
Books, Jacquard products, Stewart Gill paints

Crafty Notions
P.O. Box 6141
Newark NG24 2FQ
England
+44 01636 659890
www.craftynotions.com
Beads and bead supplies, books, Meadowbrook Industries Angelina Heat-Bondable Fiber, paints, stabilizers

Fibrecrafts & George Weil
Old Portsmouth Road
Peasmarsh, Guildford
Surrey GU3 1LZ
www.fibrecrafts.com
Books, Meadowbrook Industries Angelina Heat-Bondable Fiber, paints, workshops

Rainbow Silks
85 High Street
Great Missenden, Bucks
HP16 OAL
www.rainbowsilks.co.uk
Books, classes, Jacquard products, silk dyes, silk fabrics, stamps

Yorkshire Art Store
10 Market Place
Picering, North Yorkshire
YO18 7AA
+44 0800 195 7440
www.yorkshireartstore.co.uk
Books, Jacquard products, paints

EUROPE

Zijdelings
Kakrina van Vught
Kapelstraat 93a
5046 CL Tilburg
The Netherlands
www.zijdelings.com
Books, fabrics, Jacquard products, workshops

FURTHER READING

Creative Cloth Doll Faces
Patti Medaris Culea
Quarry Publishers
ISBN 1-59253-144-X

Creative Cloth Doll Making
Patti Medaris Culea
Rockport Publishers
ISBN 1-56496-942-8

Collage for the Soul
Holly Harrison and Paula Grasdal
Rockport Publishers
ISBN 1-56496-962-2

Fashion Design
Sue Jenkyn Jones
Watson-Guptill Publications
ISBN 0-8230-1638-2

Making Handbags
Ellen Goldstein-Lynch, Sarah Mullins, Nicole Malone
Rockport Publishers
ISBN 1-56496-849-9

Painters' Wild Workshop
Lynn Leon Loscutoff
Rockport Publishers
ISBN 1-56496-434-5

Quilted Memories
Lesley Riley
Sterling Publishers
ISBN 1-4027-1484-X

CONTRIBUTING ARTISTS

Carol Petefish Ayotte
84 Wing Boulevard West
East Sandwich, MA 02537
USA
carolayotte@adelphia.net

Born in the Midwest, Carol resided in many parts of the Unites States and Europe. She retired in 1995 after thirty-five years of teaching and supervising art and art history in public schools in the United States and military-dependent schools in Europe. She holds a bachelor of fine arts from the University of Illinois and a master of education from Towson State University in Maryland.

Since her retirement, Carol has been pursuing her life-long interest in soft-sculpture figures which combines her love of fiber arts with a longstanding interest in the plastic arts, color, and design. She has made dolls of one kind or another for most of her life.

Carol currently resides near the water on Cape Cod, with her husband, who is a retired army officer.

Darcy Balcomb
18595 Locksley Street
San Diego, CA 92128
USA
dbalcomb2002@yahoo.com

Darcy has been creating for as long as she can remember. Consistently drawn to textiles, paints, beads, and trinkets, she never thought of putting them all together to create a doll until she became a stay-at-home mom. She sells her work in galleries, teaches workshops, and has won awards for her entries in various doll exhibits. Always unusual, her one-of-a-kind creations combine many types of artistic media and involve much experimentation. She resides in San Diego with her husband and two children.

Leta Benedict
11525 SW 54 Street
Cooper City, FL 33330
USA
leta@bellsouth.net
www.letadolls.com

Born in Lancaster, California, Leta grew up the daughter of a NASA engineer and a stay-at-home mom. The extensive family traveling exposed her to many different cultures and traditions. The family settled in sunny south Florida where she met her husband and started a family. After years of sewing, sculpting, and painting Old World Santas, she was invited to join a local doll club, The Sand Doll R's. Through the club, she was exposed to many different styles and techniques, which changed her views of cloth and its limitations.

Marion Bolson
11506 Cherry Drive
Thornton, CO 80233
USA
marionbolson@comcast.net

Marion has lived in Denver, Colorado, most of her adult life. She recently celebrated her twenty-fifth wedding anniversary with her husband Mark. She has been making art dolls for about fifteen years and, last year, started selling patterns of her designs and teaching classes. Her Prayer Pocket Angel Pendant was featured in the 2005 winter issue of *Art Doll Quarterly*. She is currently the president of the Denver Doll Artisans and chairperson for the cloth and mixed media competition at the Colorado Doll and Bear Extravaganza.

Antonette Cely
3592 Cherokee Road NE
Atlanta, GA 30340-2749
USA
noni@cely.com
www.cely.com/doll/main.html

Antonette Cely is a well-known cloth doll artist whose dolls are bought by serious collectors around the world. Richard Simmons has the largest single collection of her work. Antonette has written and self-published books on doll making, including *Cloth Dollmaking*. She frequently writes for doll magazines, such as *Soft Dolls and Animals!* and *Doll Crafter*. She designed costumes and did make-up for the stage and screen for many years before turning to doll making. Her dolls are considered to be among the best in the medium of cloth. From the hand-dyed fabric used for the skin, to the internal structure that attaches each doll to her base, Antonette's meticulous attention to detail is what makes her sought after by doll makers and collectors alike. Her dolls can be seen in such books as *Here Come the Bride Dolls*, *The World's Most Beautiful Dolls*, *The Doll: By Contemporary Artists*, and *Anatomy of a Doll: The Fabric Sculptor's Handbook*, among others.

Drusilla Esslinger
3508 AA Road
Madison, KS 66860
USA
drue@madtel.net
www.drusilla.com

Dru has been making dolls for thirty years since retiring as an elementary school teacher and raising four children. She and her husband live on a farm in the middle of Flint Hills, Kansas. She teaches doll making online at www.dollstreet.com, writes articles for various magazines, and lectures. She has received several honors, including her appearance in a film documentary, *The Art of the Dollmaker*.

Diane Evdokimoff

RSM 143 Holland Road
Busselton, Western Australia 6280
Australia
fabricaddict@gmail.com

Born in Fresno, California, Diane's family migrated to Australia in the 1970s. There, she met a very supportive "guy" and together they have three children. She learned to sew by watching her mother. Even though the sewing machine was off limits to Diane, she used to sneak into the sewing room and secretly sew doll clothes. Diane believes her mother knew, but never said anything. This is where her love of sewing began. Diane is self-taught because, as she says, they "live in the back of beyond." Living in a rural setting is wonderful for raising children, but the limited access to patterns and accessories has enabled her to develop her own unique style of doll making.

Sue Farmer

10 Brookdale Avenue
Pinelands
Capetown 7405
South Africa
sufarmer@iafrica.com

Sue arrived in central Africa, from England, at the age of six. She grew up on a small holding, the only girl, with three brothers. Her mother taught her to use a treadle sewing machine and, by the age of eleven, she was able to make simple items. Sue has always found pleasure in working with fabric, so it was natural that she should drift into dressmaking, which occupied her for many years. Sue went to London to complete a diploma patternmaking course. She and her family then moved to South Africa, where she worked for the Nico Malan Opera House in Cape Town as a costumer for five years. After that, she ran own costume shop for eighteen years. She recently retired, and has been making dolls for three years.

Pam Gonzalez

14054 183rd Avenue SE
Renton, WA 98059
USA
pammster12@yahoo.com

Pam has always had a passion for sewing and creating. Encouraged by her sister, Kathy, she took a class with Elinor Peace Bailey and has been making dolls ever since. Her dolls have been featured in *Quilting Arts Magazine* and *Somerset Studio*. She received third place for Amateur Doll in the 2001 and honorable mention for Professional Doll 2004 in the Sulky Challenges. She has also won several awards for her dolls at the Western Washington Fair. When not in her studio, Pam loves doing art projects with her son, Evan.

Cody Goodin

408 Southview Avenue
Cincinnati, OH 45219
USA
codyart@fuse.net

Growing up in northern Kentucky, Cody created most of his own playthings. Though he was encouraged to pursue a "practical" line of work, Cody received undergraduate degrees in fine arts and theater design. He has been a professional artist for twenty-one years, the last fifteen as a doll maker. He makes mixed media dolls and will use any material, natural stones, crystals, feathers, beads, charms, wood, metal or recycled items for his creations. Currently he is working on mythological creatures that have their own stories. This allows him to develop another of his passions, writing.

Deb Jensen

3317 226th Place SW
Brier, WA 98036
USA
djjensen@earthlink.net

Deb has had a passion for dolls and doll clothes since childhood. It is the perfect creative outlet for her, combining her love of beading, crochet and knitting, fabric embellishment, quilting, and sewing. Working as a freelance professional writer and consultant for nonprofit organizations, Deb cherishes the time she spends in her sewing room. She is a regular contributor to *Better Homes and Gardens*, Creative Publications *Halloween Tricks and Treats, Knit It!,* and *Simply Creative Crochet,* as well as *Artisan Northwest*. She makes her home in the Pacific Northwest where she and husband Paul are the very proud parents of Chris and Whitney.

Sandra Johns
19 Pine Lane
Bremen, ME 04551
USA
edgarjohns@usadatanet.net

While living in Galesburg, Illinois, Sandra came down with encephalitis between the fifth and sixth grade. This changed her focus from an active life to one that involved working with her hands and reading.

She learned to sew while in college and began to make pillows with doll heads on them. After graduating with a teaching degree, she went on to graduate school, combining pottery and weaving in her studies. Upon completing her education, she began teaching college courses in Rockland, Illinois, and set up its textile department.

After taking a doll-making class at Penland School of Crafts, North Carolina, she got hooked on dolls. She also learned felt making there and incorporates felt into her dolls. Sandra and her husband, Edgar, live in Maine, where Edgar has built her a studio. You will find Sandra there, developing new techniques and dolls. She is now teaching and exhibiting her work and encouraging people to make dolls.

Judi Korona
3032 Dillman Drive
St. Cloud, FL 34769
USA
korona@kua.net

Judi lives in the Orlando, Florida, area and learned much of her fashion design skills while working for the Walt Disney Company. She has worked in a quilt shop called Queen Ann's Lace in Kissimmee, Florida, for many years. There, she became a Bernina expert and teaches many classes, especially on embellishing techniques using the various sewing machines in the store. She has designed for the Bernina Fashion Show. She loves doll costuming, since they wear everything well—costumes that no one would be able to wear in real life.

Sally Lampi
2261 Beckham Way
Hayward, CA 94541
USA
Slampi142@aol.com

Sally has been designing cloth doll patterns for more than twenty years. She also designs quilts and wearables. Her wonderful sense of humor and whimsy are evident in her wonderful designs. She is highly sought after as a lecturer and teacher. She lives in Hayward, California, with her husband, Bill. Most of her free time is spent with her grandchildren, who are the inspirations for many of her creations.

Dorice Larkin
19463 Oriente Drive
Yorba Linda, CA 92886
USA

Dorice comes to doll making with several skills in place, as she has five daughters. She studied textile design and theater arts in college, but her devotion to starting a family put her art on hold for many years. Her husband, Bill, and their daughters have encouraged her in her art and give her the time she needs to work in her studio. She is drawn to doll making because of the people involved in this art form, who generously share ideas as well as their stashes.

Diane Leftwich
1621 O'Connell Road
O'Connell via Bathurst NSW 2795
Australia
diane@leftwich.info

Diane has always loved textiles. Her journey in the textile arts started in knitting, designing, and selling garments in galleries. She also enjoys embroidery, felting, quilting, and shibori. Doll making has allowed to incorporate of all these textile techniques and meet other special artists. Diane is married, with two children, and is thankful to her family for putting up with her continual creative clutter and always encouraging her. She lives in natural bushland in NSW Australia, where she teaches doll making and shares her joy of textiles.

Ann Maullin
P.O. Box 106
Broke, NSW 2330
Australia
annmaullin@bigpond.com

Ann lives in the beautiful Hunter Valley of New South Wales, Australia. She has been making dolls for ten years and has traveled to the United States to teach her style of doll making. Being a figurative textile artist, she loves to create her own magical fabrics using free-motion machine embroidery and felting. She also dabbles in textile art journals and altered books.

Michelle Meinhold
1750 E. Brandon Lane
Fresno, CA 93720
USA
meinhold@csufresno.edu
www.michellemeinhold.com

Michelle Meinhold discovered her love for color while studying fine arts at the University of California, Santa Cruz. The color choices available in textiles and beads have helped fuel her creative fires. At first she used beads just to embellish her dolls. But one day, obsession took over, and beads became her medium of choice. Michelle still makes cloth dolls to satisfy her need to create. Her line of Floral Tassel dolls came into bloom when she wanted to combine the dolls with beads. She has been a cloth doll artist since 1985, and has been teaching cloth dolls and beading since 1998.

Stefania Morgante
Via Mar Ligure 36
09045 Quarto S. Elena
Cagliari, Italy
customerservice@gufobardo.com
www.gufobardo.com

Stefania is an Italian doll designer and pattern creator. Originally a painter, sculptor, and photographer, Stefania has an Arts, Music, and Show Degree. Her passion for dolls began after working as a theater editor, drawing teacher, and advertising designer. With her fabric sculptures and teddy bears, her honors include first prize at the National Teddy Bear Contest (March 2002), second prize for the Canadian Doll Artists Association (CDAA), and first prize at the National Dolls and Teddy Bears Contest (May 2005).

Michele Cokl Naylor
1904 Contention Lane
Cottonwood, AZ 86326
USA
michele@dollsbymichele.com
www.dollsbymichele.com

Michele was given a special doll by her grandmother, who had made it along with its entire wardrobe. This was her introduction to sewing. She began making dresses for her dolls and eventually those of other children. Her artistic gift has come without formal art training but by taking classes from various doll designers. She has developed her own style making contemporary art dolls with a feel for the Arizona desert where she resides. Her dolls represent people she has known, seen, or met in her imagination.

Stephanie Novatski
29 Lloyd Road
Morganville, NJ 07751
USA
novasblossoms@yahoo.com

Stephanie is a new doll maker who recently caught the attention of the cloth doll world when she won the Goblin Princess Challenge sponsored by www.Joggles.com. Her love of all things beautiful drew her to the doll world.

Nancy Palomino
40430 SE Trout Creek Road
Corbett, OR 97019
USA
palomino@cascadeaccess.com

Nancy lives in a beautiful Douglas fir forest near Portland, Oregon, with her handsome and talented husband, David. She started sewing doll clothes at the age of four and got her first machine, a treadle, at age six. She still owns it, along with seven others, and sews almost every day. About six years ago, after her two boys were grown, she started making doll clothes again, this time along with cloth dolls to wear the garments. She is a founding member of the Depot Dolls doll group, whose members inspire and encourage her.

Melinda Small Paterson
10465 NW Lee Court
Portland, OR 97229
USA
melinda@smallwork.com
www.smallwork.com

During art school, Melinda was a face painter for the Simpich Character Dolls Ltd. in Colorado, and then for ten years she built doll houses and scale wicker furniture replicas. Costuming followed, followed then by her porcelain fairy dolls and their twig furniture. That led to dragon companions made of fabric, cloth dolls, and patterns. Her doll making is inspired by folklore and mythology. It satisfies her because it combines a variety of materials and multiple skills. Knowing when to stop adding details is the hardest part for Melinda. She continues to take art courses and has been teaching doll-related classes for twenty years. For her classes, she brings layouts with samples that show every step of the process. Also, she brings her "duds" to show how each piece evolved and how many times she tried again to get what she wanted.

Elise Peeples
5508 NE 41 Avenue
Vancouver, WA 98661
USA
epeeplesdolls@comcast.net

Elise is a fiber artist who works with the human form. She employs appliqué, beading, felt making, collage, stitchery, painting, and weaving in her doll making. Her dolls have many textures, and she loves the sensual nature of fabrics and fibers, as well as the opportunities for surface design that these materials offer. While she enjoys the challenge of creating a realistic figure, her dolls tend to be quite abstract.

Elise's background is in art, dance, and theater. She is married, with two grown daughters. A recently emptied nest allows her more time to devote to her art.

Camille CS Pratt
1707 Chapelwood Lane
Richmond, TX 77469
USA
hericane@ix.netcom.com

Camille has always loved color, creativity, design, and texture. She is a self-taught artist working with many mediums. All of her skills and interests such as watercolors, writing, and reading have an impact on her primary love—doll making. Camille's work has been featured in numerous magazines and several exhibits. She teaches doll making, and enjoys sharing her knowledge to help others achieve their artistic goals.

Camille lives outside of Houston, Texas, with her patient husband and four fine daughters, each one a prolific and profound artist in her chosen medium.

Dale Rollerson
6 Smith Street
Perth 6000
Western Australia
mail@thethreadstudio.com
www.thethreadstudio.com

Dale is a teacher, textile artist, and writer living in Perth, Western Australia. Dale has been working with threads and other fibers all of her life and loves to share her ideas with others. Her dedication to textile arts led her and her husband, Ian, to start a business that specializes in hand- and machine-sewing threads, textile art supplies, and online classes. The Thread Studio is a thriving business. You will find this couple at most of the sewing and craft shows throughout Australia, and at the Knitting and Stitching Show in London, England. They plan to travel to the United States soon.

Adele Sciortino
8075 Larrey Street
Anjou, Quebec H1J 2L4
Canada
adele@artdollingetc.com
www.artdollingetc.com

Adele was born and raised in New Orleans, Louisiana, and now resides in Montreal, Quebec, Canada. Surrounded by talented family members, Adele was encouraged to follow her artistic dreams. She has studied crocheting, photography, quilting, and watercolors and has been involved in doll making for the last several years. Her works have been featured in *Soft Dolls and Animals!* and various Canadian doll publications. Her dolls have won awards both in Canada and the United States. Recently, her dolls have been on exhibit at the Venetian Resort Hotel's Casino art gallery in Las Vegas, Nevada, and at the Jack Gallery at the Seminole Hard Rock Hotel and Casino in Hollywood, Florida.

Desiree Simpson
15 Polwarth Road
Wakari
Dunedin 9001
New Zealand
desireedsimpson@hotmail.com

Desiree has always loved making things. One of her earliest memories is creating a miniature room in the garden for her fairies. Since those early days, she has dabbled in many crafts including decoupage, embroidery, folk art painting, knitting doll clothes, and sewing. She has been teaching at a quilt shop where she works for fourteen years, as well as at other venues around New Zealand. She is now designing her own patterns.

Ray Slater
36 Burrage Place
Plumstead
London SE18 7BG
UK
ray-.slater@virgin.net

Sewing has always been a part of Ray's life, from making doll clothes from the scraps of fabric left over from her mother's dressmaking, to making costumes for television and theater. She trained in embroidered textiles and theatrical costuming before working in repertory theater companies and television. She now uses her skills to create period reproduction costumes and fantasy embroidered costumes for half-scale porcelain mannequins. For the last few years, Ray has been involved with making fabric dolls and also in promoting this craft throughout the United Kingdom. She teaches in Europe and the United States.

Kathryn Thompson
67 Levens Drive
Poulton-Le-Fylde
Lancashire FY6 8EZ
UK
KathrynLThompson30@hotmail.com

From quite a young age, Kathryn Thompson has been happiest when stitching. She would use the scraps left from her mother's dressmaking and supplement them with laces and ribbons bought for a few pennies from a local bargain shop to make doll outfits. She went on from school to train as a needlework instructor, and soon began teaching in schools. Nowadays she is involved with the Embroiderers' Guild and still finds fabric, trimmings, beads, and all the wonderful methods of creating textile art a totally absorbing activity.

While on holiday in Canada in 2002, Kathryn came across a shop devoted to creative doll making. Realizing that these dolls are wonderfully expressive and a superb vehicle for a wide variety of techniques, doll making has become her favorite occupation.

Anne van der Kley
P.O. Box 98
Glenbrook, NSW 2773
Australia
sergingqueen@aol.com

Anne is one of the premiere Australian fiber artists. Known for her work with a serger, Anne has traveled the world teaching and sharing her love of manipulating threads. Anne has two published books: *Serging Australia* and *Creative Serging*, coauthored with Nancy Bednar. Recently, Anne ventured into the cloth doll world by creating what she calls "sergically enhanced" dolls.

Betts Vidal
26163 Underwood Avenue
Hayward, CA 94544
bettsbetz@aol.com

Many activites and observations led Betts to doll making. She has studied art, basketry, drawing, interior design, lapidary, quilting, painting, and pottery. She has a love of natural elements, richly textured fabrics and surfaces, luscious colors, Americana, buttons, and found objects. Doll making allows her to travel, make treasured friendships, and incorporate all of her experiences into this rewarding form of creativity. Best of all, her husband, children, grandchildren, siblings, and parents all share in her delight of dolls.

Barbara Willis
415 Palo Alto Avenue
Mountain View, CA 94041
USA
bewdolls2@aol.com
www.barbarawillisdesigns.com

Barbara has been making dolls for as long as she can remember. Designing, teaching, playing with fabric and, of course, collecting treasures for the dolls is a lifelong passion, one supported by many creative friends. She finds inspiration from life around her, and from treasures she unearths at flea markets and fabric stores. She considers herself blessed to have visited and taught in many of our fifty states and at international workshops. She continues to run a full-time design, pattern, and teaching business that is focused on cloth dolls.

ACKNOWLEDGMENTS

Completing my third book comes with a feeling of deep gratitude. I have been honored with the support of incredible artists. We have shared marvelous creations, put on happy faces, and clothed our dolls to the nth degree.

None of my books would have been completed without the help and encouragement of family and friends. I would not have been surprised if my husband, John, who helped with writing and editing, had ordered a straightjacket for me, especially as deadlines approached. When you look up the word "panic" in the dictionary, you may see my photo. As for the condition of our house, with dolls piled up and paperwork strewn about—we could have qualified for a spread in American Landfill Journal.

Thanks to Heidi, our daughter visiting from Europe, who helped me with the gown design in chapter 4. I had a total design brain block. Through her drawings and gentle encouragement, the gown came to life. Thank you, Heidi. I named the doll Christina, your middle name.

To our oldest daughter Janet, thanks for cutting out all those magazine photos of wonderful costumes and haute couture. She will recognize some of the design elements in the doll in chapter 3.

Thank you to my parents, Bob and Fran Medaris, for giving me such a creative childhood. When they saw me drawing on everything in sight, they enrolled me in art schools, starting in sixth grade. It was either that, or go broke repainting the family room walls.

Even though I almost failed sewing in school, my Aunt Willie Medaris McNally took me by the hand and made sewing fun. Thank you so much for your patience.

Thanks, also, to people like Jacinta Leischman and Dale Rollerson in Australia who taught me to go beyond the norm and experiment with fibers. Jan Beaney, from England, taught me the exciting use of heat-transfer inks. Laura McCabe, from Connecticut, guided me through the thrill of beadwork.

For the third time, huge hugs go to Mary Ann Hall of Rockport Publishers for letting me do another book. You are a great encourager.

Major smiles again for Judy Love. You took my illustrations and made sense out of them. Kudos to Roberta Frauwirth who straightened out my pattern drawings and gave them the look of a fashion professional.

One final salute to every contributing artist and also an apology to those artists whose dolls could not be used because of space limitations. Every one of your creations was simply stunning. I am humbled to have my name on the book's cover—without you, the book would have been wishful thinking.

All of this comes down to the person who reads the book. To you, please know that a whole lot of people have poured out their heart and soul to give you something we think is extra special. I wish I could see all of what you are going to do and hope that the techniques you have discovered in this book will open fantastic opportunities to stretch your artistic talent beyond what you thought was possible. God bless you all.

ABOUT THE AUTHOR

Patti Medaris Culea studied art in Los Angeles and Japan and began her career as a painter and portrait artist. Her interest in the human figure evolved into working with cloth. Today, she combines her love of silk and dyes by creating extraordinary fairies, mermaids, and other one-of-a-kind dolls. She has a full line of cloth doll patterns and her work has appeared in books, magazines, and galleries. In demand as a teacher, she travels throughout the world. She is the author of Creative Cloth Doll Making (Rockport 2003) and Creative Cloth Doll Faces (Quarry 2005). Patti lives in San Diego, California.